Macmillan Encyclopedia of the Environment

Macmillan Encyclopedia of the
ENVIRONMENT

VOLUME 1

General Editor
Stephen R. Kellert

Associate Editors
Matthew Black

Richard Haley

Macmillan Library Reference USA
New York

Developed, Designed, and Produced by Book Builders Incorporated

Copyright © 1997 by Simon & Schuster Macmillan

Macmillan Library Reference
1633 Broadway, New York, NY 10019-6785

Library of Congress Catalog Card Number: 96-29045

Printed in the United States of America

Library of Congress Cataloging-in-Publication Data

Macmillan encyclopedia of the environment.
       p.   cm.
    "General editor, Stephen R. Kellert"—P. iii.
    Includes bibliographical references and index.
    Summary: Provides basic information about such topics as minerals, energy resources, pollution, soils and erosion, wildlife and extinction, agriculture, the ocean, wilderness, hazardous wastes, population, environmental laws, ecology, and evolution.
    ISBN 0-02-897381-X (set)
    1. Environmental sciences—Dictionaries, Juvenile.
[1. Environmental protection—Dictionaries. 2. Ecology—Dictionaries.]
I. Kellert, Stephen R.   96-29045
GE10.M33 1997   CIP
333.7—dc20   AC

Photo credits are gratefully acknowledged in a special listing in Volume 6, page 102.

Contents

Preface   vii

Introduction   ix

Macmillan Encyclopedia of the Environment

The following resources may be found in Volume 6:

Major Environmental Events and
Legislation in the United States   79

Environmental Organizations   84

U.S. Government Organizations
with Environmental Responsibility   95

Selected Bibliography   97

Subject Index   106

General Index   111

Preface

The environment, as a field of study, is relatively young. People have, of course, always been concerned about nature, but the scientific study and conservation of the natural environment did not really begin in an organized and active way until the end of the nineteenth century. One of the major turning points was the establishment of the world's first national park, Yellowstone, in 1872. However, America did not start to protect its forests, wildlife, waters, soils, and other natural resources, or even use them wisely and conservatively, until the twentieth century. The United States is only now acquiring the knowledge, tools, and policies needed to ensure the long-term protection of the natural environment. Many other countries, especially in the developing world, are just beginning this process.

The modern world faces many environmental problems and challenges. Three major areas of difficulty stand out: various kinds of pollution of air, water, and other substances; the overuse of many natural resources, including oil, forests, and aquatic animals; and the extinction of species, including the general reduction in the number of many types of plants and animals. Considerable knowledge, as well as effective new laws and regulations, will be required to deal with these problems in a timely way.

The *Macmillan Encyclopedia of the Environment* provides basic information about important topics that span the subject of conservation and the laws designed to protect our natural environment. The *Encyclopedia* contains almost 600 entries covering a wide range of subjects. It includes topics relating to minerals and energy resources, the atmosphere and air pollution, water and water pollution, soils and soil erosion, forests and forestry, wildlife and extinction, agriculture and pesticides, the ocean and fisheries, parks and wilderness, solid and hazardous wastes, population and its effect on the environment, various environmental laws and regulations, and ecology and evolution. At the end of Volume 6, readers will find a helpful resource section that lists major environmental events and legislation, the names and addresses of various environmental organizations, government agencies with environmental responsibility, and a selected bibliography of useful books on the subject. The resource section is followed by a subject index and the comprehensive general index. Another useful feature of the *Encyclopedia* is the inclusion of more than 1,000 photographs and illustrations. Entries are arranged alphabetically, and numerous cross-references will aid the reader in locating related entries throughout the six volumes.

A project of this size requires the assistance of many people. I particularly wish to thank my co-editors, Matthew Black, resident naturalist of the Connecticut Audubon Coastal Center, and Richard Haley, currently director of the Goodwin Conservation Center, for their intelligent contributions. Special thanks are due also to the advisory board members, whose names are listed at the front of these volumes, as well as to Elly Dickason, publisher of Macmillan Library Reference. Finally, I want to recognize the teams of writers, researchers, editors, copy editors, illustrators, and photo researchers guided by Book Builders Incorporated, particularly Beatrice Jacinto, the project's managing editor; Lauren Fedorko, the company's president; and Shirley Chetter, the company's design and production director.

The effective conservation and protection of our natural environment will require informed, appreciative, and concerned citizens. Awareness and appreciation of the significance of the environment begin at an early age. This *Encyclopedia* offers basic knowledge to its young readers on the environment and its conservation and is a necessary reference guide that will point the way toward obtaining additional information about the timely topic of preserving our natural world.

STEPHEN R. KELLERT

Introduction

The environment provides humans with food, water, medicine, energy, and other resources that are basic necessities for life. While the preservation and protection of the environment have been recognized issues for more than a century, they are more crucial today than ever before. The last fifty years have seen the development of unprecedented environmental problems on a global scale, including the extinction of species at a greater rate than at any other point in human experience, the wearing down of the earth's protective ozone layer, and an increase in the release of harmful industrial chemicals into the air and water.

The *Macmillan Encyclopedia of the Environment* offers almost 600 useful and informative articles about how the environment works and how people relate to the natural world. Because human interaction with the environment has often included abuse of the natural world, the *Encyclopedia* also focuses on the ways in which people have responded to this, the passage of laws to protect the environment, and the development of new technologies to preserve it.

The environment includes just about everything around us. *Merriam Webster's Collegiate Dictionary* (10th edition) defines the environment as "the circumstances, objects, or conditions by which one is surrounded." The focus of the *Encyclopedia,* however, is much more selective. Its emphasis is on the physical and biological factors of the natural world, the elements that influence living conditions for humans and other species of life. Air, water, minerals, rocks, soils, plants, animals, and other basic features of the natural world all work together to affect the human condition. In turn, human interaction with nature sometimes disturbs the natural environment. The *Encyclopedia* helps to enumerate which tools, laws, and policies have been developed to protect that environment.

In a comprehensive approach, the *Encyclopedia* delivers information in four major areas. It first seeks to provide basic facts about the natural world and how it functions and is structured. There are entries covering ecology, evolution, the earth, and natural cycles, with definitions of key concepts such as ecosystems, habitat, extinction, natural selection, oxygen cycles, and nitrogen cycles. Also discussed are the properties of natural resources such as the atmosphere, oceans, fresh water, soils, minerals, forests, and wildlife. Entries on wildlife consider the characteristics of mammals, birds, reptiles, amphibians, fish, and insects and other invertebrates. Interesting discussions about environmental concerns focus on such animals as the bald eagle, giant panda, and elephant. Other wildlife topics include biodiversity, endangered species, and hunting.

The *Encyclopedia*'s second area of information is an exploration of human interaction with nature, including the ways in which people use, and sometimes abuse, the environment, and the resulting problems. Articles explore the use of water for drinking and agriculture, forests for timber and paper, minerals for energy and consumer products, and grasslands for livestock and mining. Problems arising from the excessive use, or exploitation, of natural resources include air and water pollution, soil erosion and contamination, solid and hazardous wastes, forest destruction, the endangerment and extinction of species, and other harmful conditions, all of which can be compounded by the roles of human population growth, consumption, economics, and technology.

The *Encyclopedia*'s third area of principal concern is to provide information about the methods and laws that have been developed to conserve nature and to solve the environmental problems that result from overuse and abuse of the natural world. Noted policies and technologies focusing on conservation, as well as government agencies given the responsibility of carrying out these policies, are described. Some of the pivotal environmental protection laws treated by the *Encyclopedia* include the Clean Air and Water Acts, the National Environmental Policy Act, the Solid Waste Disposal Act, the Hazardous Substances Act, the Endangered Species Act, the Safe Drinking Water Act, Superfund, and a host of other statutes and regulations. Instrumental in protection are government agencies such as the Environmental Protection Agency, the National Park Service, the Department of Agriculture, the Department of the Interior, and many others found in the United States and all over the world. The tools employed by these various organizations include the creation of national parks and other protected areas, the conservation of endangered species, the use of environmental impact statements, the development of techniques for controlling hazardous wastes, the treatment of drinking water, and the control of air pollution.

Finally, the *Encyclopedia* considers our economic and ethical relationships with nature. Various entries discuss strategies for promoting economic prosperity while protecting the natural environment, and others present the importance of human values and ethics in the conservation of nature. Among the people cited as having contributed much to environmental protection are Aldo Leopold, Rachel Carson, Dian Fossey, John Muir, Ruth Patrick, and Gifford Pinchot.

During the past two centuries, and particularly since the mid-1970s, people have realized that there is a great deal to learn about the way in which nature functions and about its attendant environmental problems. This has created a change in our understanding of the natural world as well as a reassessment of our ability to protect it. Only at the end of the last century did the need to protect nature become a prominent issue in the United States. The historical development of this field has since passed through three broad stages.

In the first historical period—toward the end of the nineteenth and beginning of the twentieth centuries—the major emphasis of the field of environmental science was on the conservation and wise use of natural resources. This concern stemmed largely from the excessive and often destructive use of America's natural resources during the nation's pioneering period. Environmentalists were not alone in realizing that this exploitation of the country's forests, wildlife, minerals, and other resources would eventually lead to great scarcities and environmental damage. As a consequence, new laws and methodologies arose to ensure the future availability of the nation's natural resources, as well as to identify certain areas for permanent protection. America's first national parks were created during this period, along with a system of national forests and wildlife refuges. In addition, pioneering policies and techniques were established to manage and conserve natural resources more effectively.

The second historical period of environmental science developed largely after World War II, when people became increasingly aware of the pollution of air, water, and soil, as well as the spread of hazardous and toxic materials into the environment. This time was marked by a new recognition that pollutants could threaten human health and well-being. The pioneering work of Rachel Carson and others brought to the nation's attention the idea that modern industry and technology could significantly contaminate the environment and damage basic life-support systems and processes. As a result, new laws and pollution-control methodologies were conceived to protect the health and safety of people and the natural world.

The third historical period, the present stage of environmental awareness, reflects an increasing realization that numerous environmental problems occur on a global scale. For example, some disturbances in the earth's atmosphere have been associated with the spread of industrial chemicals, such as chlorofluorocarbons (CFCs). The burning of the earth's sheltering ozone layer results in increases in carbon dioxide in the atmosphere, indicating possible global warming and planetary climate change. Another problem that occurs on a global scale has been the loss of thousands of species, resulting from the widespread destruction of tropical rain forests and other natural areas in the world. The current rate of extinction is comparable to only a few periods in the history of life on earth.

These problems have resulted largely from dramatic increases in human population, the impact of new technologies expanding worldwide trade and consumption, and the excessive use and depletion of energy resources. Human population, for example, has roughly doubled during the past half century to more than 5.5 billion. Directly or indirectly, people use more than forty percent of the living energy produced by the sun each year.

Efforts to solve these global environmental problems require international cooperation and assistance as well as new policies, technologies, and a change in attitude toward nature. Ideally, policies will seek to ensure economic prosperity while maintaining a healthy environment, and innovative technologies will focus on controlling pollution and encouraging the rehabilitation of damaged natural systems. Most of all, people will have to alter historical attitudes and assumptions about the natural world. We need to recognize that a world of natural health and beauty is essential for productive human societies and political security. Humans can only prosper if they live compatibly with nature.

The human race is at a pivotal point in its relationship with the natural world. Although we face environmental problems that present unprecedented environmental challenges, we also possess the tools and interest for dealing with these problems. The role of young people in facing these challenges to our existence will be critical. The health and productivity of the natural world depends on the information we gather and the choices we make.

A

Abiotic Factors

The nonliving features of an ENVIRONMENT. Examples are water, light, temperature, air, SOIL, and **inorganic** nutrients. Like the living organisms of the environment, abiotic factors are an important part of a functioning ECOSYSTEM.

These abiotic factors of the environment shape ecosystems in many ways. Such factors influence the diversity and distribution of organisms, as well as their feeding, growth, reproduction, and metabolism. Organisms interact with abiotic factors in search of food, heat, light, shelter, air, and water.

Perhaps the most important abiotic factor is water. All organisms need water in order to survive. PLANTS need water for PHOTOSYNTHESIS. Water is the main component of cells and of the fluids that bathe cells, providing an environment in which the chemical reactions that sustain cells can take place. It is also an important medium in which many organisms live and reproduce.

Because water is so crucial to life, its availability has a major impact on the types of organisms that can live in a particular environment. Any factor of the environment that has a significant role in supporting organisms is considered a limiting factor. Thus, water is a limiting factor in many environments. For instance, in areas that receive 30–100 inches (75–250 centimeters) of rainfall per year, DECIDUOUS FORESTS—populated by large, leafy trees, shrubs, and other plants—are common. In contrast, regions that receive a maximum of 10 inches (25 centimeters) of rain annually are DESERTS. Deserts have sparse vegetation that is adapted to survival in dry areas. The few plants that can survive in this type of environment obtain and conserve the small amounts of water available to them.

Light, another essential abiotic factor, is the original source of energy for so many organisms. Through the process of photosynthesis, plants and most other PRODUCERS change the energy in sunlight into chemical energy that can be used by most organisms. Light has important effects on the distribution and adaptations of many organisms, particularly producers. For instance, light can penetrate deep into ecosystems where few plants grow. In contrast, in nutrient-rich ecosystems, such as deciduous forests, light becomes a factor that limits growth on the forest floor. Similarly, in tropical RAIN FORESTS where the thick branches and leaves of large trees block the sun, many plants, such as **bromeliads** and mosses, must grow on tree branches to receive ample sunlight. In aquatic, or water, ecosystems, most species of ALGAE live near the surface of the water because light cannot penetrate very deep into water.

In general, temperature is affected by altitude and latitude. Temperature tends to decrease as altitude increases, or as one moves away from Earth's surface. Similarly, temperature generally decreases as one moves farther north or south of the equator. All organisms are adapted to survive within particular temperature ranges. For example, the types of organisms that live in northern Canada or in mountainous areas are very different from those living in Brazil or in valleys.

Terrestrial organisms depend on soil in a great variety of ways. Countless microscopic organisms such as BACTERIA, protists, and FUNGI live in the soil. Soil also provides HABITAT to larger SPECIES, such as worms, moles, and snakes. Plants rely on soil as a source of water, MINERALS, and the other nutrients they require.

THE LANGUAGE OF THE ENVIRONMENT

bromeliads a family of non-woody, usually tropical plants that include pineapples and Spanish moss.

inorganic of or relating to substances that lack carbon and are not formed by living things.

terrestrial living on the land.

Water

Soil

◆ Abiotic factors in the environment influence the distribution and variety of organisms in many ways

Light

Temperature

For soil-supported organisms, especially plants, the quality of soil is important. Plants are adapted to grow in many different soils. Desert plants, such as cacti, for instance, are adapted to survive in dry, sandy soils. In contrast, wetlands plants grow better in moist soils. [*See also* BIOME; CLIMATE; and WATER QUALITY STANDARDS.]

Acid Precipitation

See ACID RAIN

Acid Rain

⏸ PRECIPITATION that has a lower pH than normal. Acid rain, along with other acid precipitation, can have significant effects on WILDLIFE. Acid rain is often seen in rural areas surrounding major cities. The northeastern United States and northern Europe have been hit hardest by this problem.

The main causes of acid rain are AUTOMOBILES, factories, power plants, and other sources of pollutants that form from the burning of FOSSIL FUELS. When fossil fuels, such as gasoline, oil, and COAL, are burned, they release SULFUR DIOXIDE and NITROGEN OXIDES as **by-products**. In the ATMOSPHERE, these pollutants can combine with water and other chemicals to form nitric acid

◆ Acid rain can cause stone structures, such as statues, to dissolve.

and sulfuric acid. When the acidified water falls to Earth as rain, snow, sleet, fog, or dew, we call it *acid precipitation.*

HOW STRONG IS ACID RAIN?

The strength of acid rain is determined by its pH. The pH of a solution is a measurement of how acidic the solution is. All rain contains some acid. Normal, unpolluted rain has a pH between 5.0 and 5.6. By contrast, acid rain usually has a pH range of 4.0 to 5.0. In highly industrialized regions, the pH of acid rain can be very acidic. With pH readings below 4.0, the acid rain in these areas can be as strong as vinegar (3.3) and sometimes even lemon juice (2.3).

HOW ACID RAIN AFFECTS ECOSYSTEMS

When acid rain falls, it can produce many problems for the ENVIRONMENT, particularly for FORESTS and aquatic ECOSYSTEMS. All aquatic organisms are adapted to survive within particular pH ranges. Most freshwater FISH, for instance, survive best within a pH range of 5.0 to 6.0. When acid rain falls on a lake, it changes the pH of the water, killing many aquatic animals, PLANTS, and other creatures.

The most immediate consequence of acid rainfall on an area is an increased acidity of the surrounding land and water. The effects can be very bad in the spring, after the melting of acid snow that has accumulated during winter. The melted snow flows into lakes, rivers, and streams, causing a sudden increase in the acidity of the waters.

This influx of acid greatly affects wildlife, particularly fish and AMPHIBIANS. Spring is breeding time for these organisms, and the

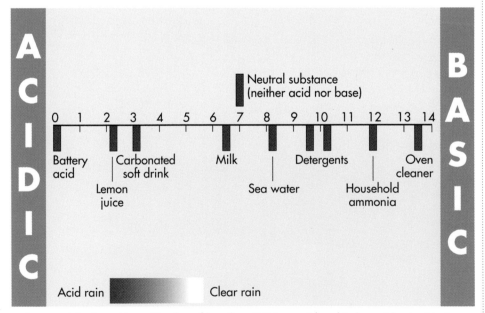

Neutral substance (neither acid nor base)

| 0 | 1 | 2 | 3 | 4 | 5 | 6 | 7 | 8 | 9 | 10 | 11 | 12 | 13 | 14 |

Battery acid | Lemon juice | Carbonated soft drink | Milk | Sea water | Detergents | Household ammonia | Oven cleaner

Acid rain — Clear rain

◆ Any precipitation with a pH value of less than 5.0 is considered to be acid rain. Most acid rain has a pH range of 4.0–5.0, but it can be even more acidic and have a lower pH.

increased acidity interferes with their reproduction. They tend to produce fewer eggs, most of which never hatch. The offspring that do hatch are usually weak or ill and cannot survive for very long.

The effects of acid rain on vegetation can be just as dramatic. When plants absorb acidic water through their roots, they gradually die. As plants die, the animals they support eventually die as well. Acid rain has already played a role in the decline of vast stretches of forest in northern Europe, the northeastern United States, and parts of Canada.

The **depletion** of nutrients from the SOIL is a long-term consequence of acid rain. When acids accumulate, important nutrients, such as calcium, magnesium, and potassium, are depleted from the soil, making the environment less fertile for plants. Acid rain can also cause dangerous substances, such as ALUMINUM, to be released from the soil. Aluminum can be very harmful to wildlife, particularly fish. Aluminum can build up on a fish's gills, leading to blockage and eventual suffocation of the fish.

Scientists are also concerned about the effects of acid rain on human-made structures, such as buildings, bridges, monuments, and statues. Acid rain dissolves the chemicals in concrete and limestone. Today, many of the world's most historic monuments and statues are being destroyed by acid rain.

CONTROLLING ACID RAIN

Acid rain can be controlled in several ways. The most obvious way

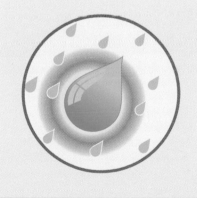

◆ Acid rain can be very damaging to forests and the animals that they support.

is to reduce the emission of sulfur dioxide and nitrogen oxides into the air. Today, laws require that the smokestacks of factories and power plants be equipped with SCRUBBERS, pollution-control devices that can cleanse emissions of harmful substances. Likewise, all automobiles must now be equipped with CATALYTIC CONVERTERS, which change dangerous nitrogen oxides into a less harmful form of nitrogen. To counteract the effects of acid rain, many states and countries also spread powdered lime over lakes and ponds and around trees. Lime is alkaline, which means it has a pH above 7. Lime neutralizes the acids in the water and returns the water to a more normal pH range (around 7).

One of the biggest obstacles to controlling acid rain is that pollutants released in one area can fall as acid rain in other areas hundreds of miles away. For instance,

because of wind and weather patterns, the acid rain in the New England region of the United States and southern Canada originates from the industrialized states of the midwestern and eastern United States. Similarly, the acid rain that falls in the Scandinavian countries of northern Europe results from pollution produced in central Germany.

Controlling acid rain requires international cooperation. In 1989, the United States, along with 27 other nations, signed the United Nations Sofia Agreement, which requires a reduction in nitrogen oxide emissions. In 1990, congressional amendments to the U.S. CLEAN AIR ACT included provisions for significantly reducing industrial emissions of sulfur dioxide and nitrogen oxides by the year 2000. [*See also* AIR POLLUTION; POLLUTION; PRIMARY POLLUTION; and WEATHERING.]

Adaptation

▌A characteristic or behavior that helps a SPECIES survive in its ENVIRONMENT. All living things must be able to grow, reproduce, and adjust to changes in the environment. For example, animals must be able to find shelter and obtain food and water and, in some cases, defend themselves from PREDATORS. PLANTS must be able to capture sunlight and obtain the water and MINERALS they need from SOIL. Through the process of NATURAL SELECTION, organisms **evolve** adaptations that help them carry out these life processes.

Often the adaptations organisms use for survival are physical structures. For example, the sharp, pointed teeth of dogs and cats are adaptations for grasping and tear-

ing the meat that is part of their diets. The broad, flat leaves of many plants are adaptations for trapping sunlight.

TYPES OF ADAPTATIONS

Individual organisms have many different adaptations that interact and work together to form a functioning organism. The shape of a fish's body, the length of its fins, the speed at which it swims, and its ability to adjust to temperature changes in the water are adaptations that must work together to help a fish survive in its HABITAT. Scientists classify adaptations by type.

Structural Adaptations

The most apparent adaptations are traits that involve an organism's structure or anatomy. Traits such as the shape of a plant's leaves, the length of a bird's beak, and the shape of a monkey's hand are examples of structural adaptations.

Many structural adaptations in animals are for obtaining food. For instance, the long, narrow tongue of a woodpecker is an adaptation for picking out insects that live beneath the bark of a tree. Similarly, the long, sticky tongue of an anteater is a structural adaptation for catching ants that live deep within anthills.

Many structural adaptations evolve in internal rather than external structures. The thick walls of the arteries in your body are adaptations for circulating blood throughout the body. The long length of your small intestine is an adaptation for absorbing the nutrients needed by your body.

Physiological Adaptations

Some adaptations are physiological. Such adaptations are associated

◆ The giraffe's long neck is an example of a structural adaptation.

◆ All organisms possess adaptations for surviving in their environment. Anteaters have long, pointy snouts and sticky tongues for catching the ants that they use for food.

◆ The California pitcher plant has modified leaves that entrap insects, which are then digested and partly absorbed.

with the functions of the cells, tissues, and organs of organisms. Many physiological adaptations involve chemical processes. For instance, plants contain a chemical called *chlorophyll.* Chlorophyll is an adaptation for the food-making process of PHOTOSYNTHESIS. In animals, physiological adaptations include chemicals that aid in digestion, the clotting of blood, and the contraction of muscles.

Behavioral Adaptations

The **behavior** of an organism is also an adaptation to its environment. For example, many birds and other animals migrate seasonally in search of food. Lions and other predatory cats engage in group HUNTING. Plants also have behavioral adaptations. For example, the bending of stems or turning of leaves toward light is a behavioral adaptation of plants. Behavioral adaptations allow organisms to respond to changes in their environment.

INTERACTIONS OF ADAPTATIONS

Scientists often study adaptations separately. However, classifying adaptations is an artificial process. In nature, adaptations interact with and depend on each other to keep an organism alive. For example, the hunting behavior of a cheetah can be classified as a behavioral adaptation. However, this behavior cannot occur without a set of structural adaptations the cheetah has developed. The structural adaptations include a flexible spine, powerful leg muscles, and large paws. Hunting also requires the inter-

actions of many physiological adaptations, such as impulses from the brain that signal muscles to contract and the work done by the cells to provide the energy needed for running.

ORIGINS OF ADAPTATIONS

Adaptations arise in a population as variations increase in frequency. A variation is a slight difference in the appearance of a trait. For example, variations in humans include differences in height, weight, eye color, and hair color.

Variations are the raw materials on which natural selection acts. If a variation makes an individual organism better suited for a particular environment, natural selection will tend to favor that variation.

Favorable variations increase an individual's chances for surviving and reproducing in a particular environment. In contrast, individuals with unfavorable variations may not survive or live to reproductive age.

When organisms reproduce, favorable variations are passed on to offspring. Over time, all members of a population have the variation. When all members of the population have the variation, it becomes an adaptation. Thus, adaptations are products of EVOLUTION through natural selection. [*See also* ADAPTIVE RADIATION; CONVERGENT EVOLUTION; DARWIN, CHARLES ROBERT; and GENETICS.]

Adaptive Radiation

The EVOLUTION of several new SPECIES from a single, ancestral species. Species that evolve through adaptive radiation have behavioral or structural ADAPTATIONS that differ from those of their predecessors. These adaptations enable the new species to survive in a HABITAT or NICHE that differs from those of the ancestral species. The evolution of new species through adaptive radiation occurs as a result of COMPETITION.

In nature, organisms sharing the same ECOSYSTEM are in competition with each other for the resources the ecosystem provides. For example, PLANTS compete with each other for water, nutrients, and available sunlight. Animals compete with each other for food, living space, and suitable habitats for reproduction and the raising of young. Such competition requires organisms of the same species to spread out over as large an area as possible to obtain the resources they need or to make use of individual variations in traits that enable them to surpass others of their species. Through the process of NATURAL SELECTION, organisms develop successful strategies for surviving in their ENVIRONMENT and pass their successful traits to their offspring. Over time, these offspring may differ enough from the ancestral species to evolve into a completely new species.

The 14 species of finches observed by Charles DARWIN on the GALÁPAGOS ISLANDS provide a good example of adaptive radiation. After observing these finches, Darwin concluded that they had all evolved from a single species of ground-dwelling, seed-eating finch. He hypothesized that the 14 different species of finches, each with slightly differently shaped beaks and feet suited to obtaining different types of foods, had evolved through the process of natural selection. [*See also* BIODIVERSITY and CONVERGENT EVOLUTION.]

Aerobic

Requiring, using, or containing molecular OXYGEN (O_2). Aerobic organisms are those that require oxygen to carry out their life functions and to survive. Such organisms include MAMMALS, other animals, PLANTS, and many types of BACTERIA. The ATMOSPHERE, as well as bodies of water that contain DISSOLVED OXYGEN, such as OCEANS and lakes, are aerobic ENVIRONMENTS. Aerobic organisms use this oxygen for RESPIRATION and other biochemical processes. Many DECOMPOSITION processes are also aerobic. [*See also* BIOCHEMICAL OXYGEN DEMAND (BOD); EUTROPHICATION; OXYGEN CYCLE; and WATER POLLUTION.]

Aerosol

Liquid droplets, solid particles, and a mixture of liquids and solids suspended in air. Aerosols serve as microscopic particles for the formation of rain droplets, fog, and CLOUDS.

Moisture in the air is constantly mixing with tiny bits of soot, SOIL, smoke, dust, and pollen to produce aerosols in the ATMOSPHERE. These aerosols promote AIR POLLUTION. Aerosols in the atmosphere reflect some of the sun's RADIATION back into space. This action helps reduce the amount of sunlight that reaches Earth's surface. The red glow in the sky at sunset is caused by atmospheric aerosols scattering the sun's light.

Commercial aerosol cans are used for many products. Among them are spray paints, antiseptics, and cosmetics. The product inside the can is dissolved in a gas propellant. Then the can is sealed under pressure. When the button on the can is pushed, a release valve opens and the compressed solution sprays out in a fine mist, which contains chemicals that can stay in the air long after they are released.

Chlorofluorocarbons (CFCs) are chemicals that have been used as propellants in some spray cans and as coolants in air conditioners and refrigerators. These chemicals pollute the air as they drift slowly up into the STRATOSPHERE. Once CFCs reach the stratosphere, they break down in reaction to the sun's ultraviolet rays. As CFCs break down, they produce chemicals that destroy the OZONE LAYER, Earth's protective shield against the sun's damaging radiation.

In 1978, the government of the United States banned the use of some CFCs because of their potential danger. However, scientists have determined that CFCs can remain in the atmosphere for more than 100 years. Many scientists are researching safe ways to destroy the CFCs that are now in the air. In addition, these scientists have continued working to find chemicals that can be used in products in place of CFCs. In June of 1990, representatives from 93 nations, including the United States, agreed to phase out the production of CFCs and other depleting chemicals by the beginning of the twenty-first century. [*See also* OZONE and OZONE HOLE.]

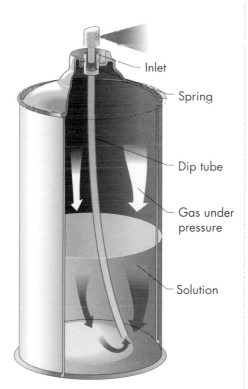

◆ An aerosol can keeps its contents under pressure until a valve is pressed that releases the propellant gas and some of the product into the air.

Age Structure

▶ A description of the population makeup of an area, usually a country, according to the ages of its people. DEMOGRAPHY is the study of populations and their characteristics.

One concern of demography is the age structure of populations. This information is usually reported in age ranges that represent periods of five to ten years. The data may be further broken down to show the number of males and females in each age group.

Age structure analyses are made for specific areas, usually a country or a large city. By analyzing the age structure of an area, researchers can make predictions about the area's needs, problems,

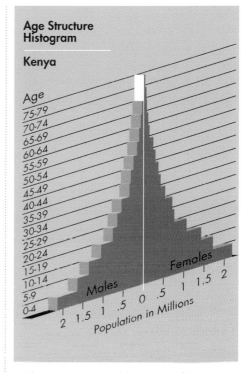

◆ The age structure histogram of Kenya shows a population that is likely to grow.

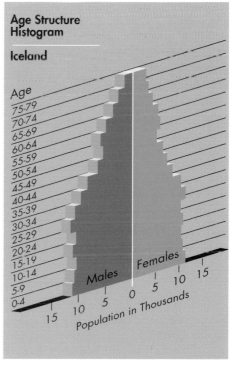

◆ The histogram of Iceland shows a population that is likely to remain stable.

and impact on the ENVIRONMENT. For example, if the age structure of an area shows that the elderly population will rise, medical and housing facilities that can meet the needs of this growing population may be constructed. Similarly, if the population of children under age 5 suddenly decreases, an area may anticipate the need to close some schools. In addition, jobs may need to be created in other fields for school workers who may face unemployment.

The age structure of a population is often shown in a graph called a *histogram.* A histogram is a bar graph that shows the age distribution of a country's population. The number of males and females in each age group is clearly shown on either side of the histogram. Thus, the histogram provides a kind of snapshot of the age structure of the population at any given time.

The histogram is usually created after a census has been taken. In the age structure histograms for Kenya and Iceland shown in the previous page, one can see that most of the people in Kenya are under 20 years of age. Thus, the population is likely to grow rapidly as these young people begin to have children. The histogram of Iceland, on the other hand, shows that the population is stable. There are approximately the same number of people in all age groups up to age 40. By looking carefully at the age structure histograms, demographers can determine the potential needs and problems of each country. [*See also* POPULATION GROWTH.]

Agricultural Pollution

The release of harmful substances into the ENVIRONMENT as a result of farming or ranching practices. Agriculture is the raising of crops and animals, mostly for the production of food and food products. Virtually all nations of the world rely on some form of agriculture to provide their peoples and the peoples of other nations with a constant food supply. Although it is clear that the human population of the world could not survive without the products of agriculture, it is also clear that many agricultural practices produce pollutants that threaten the environment. These pollutants result mostly from three conditions: EROSION of TOPSOIL, the use of fertilizers, and the use of PESTICIDES.

TOPSOIL EROSION

When left uncovered, topsoil is easily carried away by such agents as wind and running water. Silt, the smallest and lightest SOIL particles, can be carried great distances by the wind. In the air, silt is a pollutant that can irritate the eyes and respiratory system. However, silt and other soil particles carried by wind and water are eventually deposited on land or in bodies of water. The dropping of these SEDIMENTS can be beneficial to the environment by providing new soil for the growth of PLANTS. However, if silt is deposited in large amounts in ponds, lakes, streams, or the OCEAN,

it can remain suspended in the water. In some cases, large amounts of silt in the water can disrupt the functioning of the ECOSYSTEM by preventing sunlight from penetrating the water. Without sunlight, ALGAE and plants living in the water are unable to carry out PHOTOSYNTHESIS and therefore die. In addition, fine particles of silt may be taken into the respiratory or digestive systems of organisms living in the water, making the organisms unable to carry out these vital life processes.

Over time, some soil particles carried into bodies of water may settle to the bottom. This process is called SEDIMENTATION. Sedimentation can provide nutrient-rich soil in which pond plants can take root. However, over time, if too much sediment is deposited, the entire ecosystem could be changed through the process of SUCCESSION into another type of ecosystem. For example, a lake or pond ecosystem may be slowly changed to a swamp or bog. This occurs as deposited sediment builds up, making water shallower, while at the same time allowing many more plants to grow in the lake.

THE USE OF FERTILIZERS

Fertilizers are chemicals that are added to soil to replace nutrients that are removed by plants. Although the use of fertilizers is designed to promote plant growth, some environmental problems may be caused by fertilizers that are washed out of the soil and into **aquatic** ecosystems.

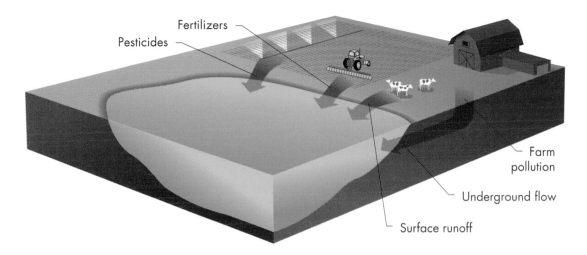

Fertilizers

Pesticides

Farm pollution

Underground flow

Surface runoff

◆ When nutrient-rich fertilizers from farms are washed into a nearby body of water, they can bring about an excessive growth of algae. This condition is called an *algal bloom.*

The most significant problem associated with fertilizers in aquatic ecosystems is EUTROPHICATION. Eutrophication is the accumulation of nutrients in pond or lake water. Once in the water, these nutrients are absorbed by algae and plants living in the water. Often these nutrients promote so much growth that a population explosion called an ALGAL BLOOM occurs. During an algal bloom, the pond or lake becomes "choked" by the excessive growth of algae. When the algae population becomes too great for the ecosystem to support, many algae begin to die and their remains drift to the bottom of the lake or pond. As BACTERIA and other DECOM-POSERS begin breaking down the dead algae, large amounts of OXYGEN dissolved in the water are used up by these organisms. This significantly lowers the DISSOLVED OXYGEN content of the water, making it unable to support fish and other organisms. Thus, an ecosystem that was once teeming with life becomes unable to support life.

The raising of LIVESTOCK, such as cattle, may also cause the same problems to aquatic ecosystems as do fertilizers. Cow manure has long been used as a natural fertilizer because it is rich in nitrates. On some commercial cattle ranches, cattle are fed in areas called *feedlots*. As the manure produced by the cattle builds up, rainwater may wash the nitrates into ponds or lakes, causing an algal bloom.

THE USE OF PESTICIDES

PESTICIDES are chemical compounds that are used to rid an area of unwanted organisms such as weeds, INSECTS, bacteria, and FUNGI. Such chemicals are often sprayed on crops to prevent damage by organisms. The use of pesticides creates several problems for people and ecosystems.

Pesticide Poisoning and Sickness

Pesticides are designed to kill certain types of organisms. However, pesticides often directly sicken or kill organisms other than those intended. For example, insects that are actually helpful to farmers because of their roles in POLLINATION may be killed by a pesticide that is intended to kill another type of insect. In addition, many pesticides can cause sickness or even death in people who come in direct contact with them. Exposure to some types of pesticides has also been linked to CANCER.

Bioaccumulation of Pesticides

Many pesticides do not break down quickly in the environment. Over time, these pesticides can

◆ Spreading fertilizers to replace nutrients in the soil sometimes causes pollution in nearby lakes or streams.

accumulate in water, soil, or even the tissues of organisms. One of the best known examples of this accumulating effect occurred with a substance known as dichlorodiphenyl trichloroethane (DDT.) During the 1940s and 1950s, DDT was one of the most commonly used pesticides in the United States. However, it was later discovered that through the process of BIOACCUMULATION, DDT was causing some BIRDS to lay eggs that had very thin shells. As a result of the thin shells, the eggs broke before the embryos inside fully developed. Thus, populations of birds, such as the BALD EAGLE, that were affected by DDT were decreasing in size because new birds were not being born to replace those that died. Because of this unexpected side effect, the use of DDT in the United States was banned in 1972. However, DDT and other harmful pesticides continue to be used in many other countries of the world.

Resistance to Pesticides

A problem associated with repeated use of pesticides is that the organisms the pesticides are designed to kill often develop a **resistance** to the chemicals in the pesticides. As a result, the pesticides become ineffective, which makes it necessary to use newer and stronger pesticides or other methods of pest control.

SOLUTIONS TO AGRICULTURAL POLLUTION PROBLEMS

To help reduce some of the pollution problems associated with agriculture, many farmers have begun practicing farming methods that are more environmentally friendly. For example, farmers often practice CONSERVATION and farming methods to prevent topsoil erosion. Such methods may include planting trees around their farms to reduce the strength of winds blowing over their fields and keeping some type of plant cover on the ground throughout the year. Other farming methods such as CONTOUR FARMING, TERRACING, and strip-cropping also help reduce the effects of erosion.

Farmers have discovered that the plowing that loosens soil also makes it more prone to erosion. Thus, many farmers have reduced the amount of plowing that takes place on their fields. Some farmers have begun to use a farming method called NO-TILL AGRICULTURE, in which a special machine digs a small hole, deposits seeds into it, then fertilizes and covers it, all without plowing. This method of farming reduces time, lessens the risk of erosion, and places fertilizers exactly where they are needed, right at the root of the developing plant.

To help reduce the problems caused by fertilizers, many farmers are using methods that lessen the need to add additional fertilizers to soil. One method farmers sometimes use is CROP ROTATION. In crop rotation, the same crops are not planted in the same fields in successive years. Instead, a crop that was planted in one field during one year is moved to another field during the next growing season. Because different crops remove different nutrients from the soil, the movement of crops from one area to another helps prevent the complete removal of certain nutrients from a certain area of soil. Also, some plants, such as LEGUMES, help to replace nutrients removed from the soil by other plants. If these plants are periodically grown in areas where other types of plants once stood, soil nutrients are replaced through natural methods.

One type of pest control that is being considered as an alternative to pesticides is a practice known as INTEGRATED PEST MANAGEMENT (IPM). This practice combines the ideas of crop diversity and the use of living organisms to control unwanted pest populations. By planting a variety of crops, farmers do not create an environment that supports unlimited growth of certain types of pests, such as insects, fungi, bacteria, or VIRUSES. Instead, the mix of crops reduces the chances that a pest organism will find the food source it needs to survive. In addition, farmers may also release into their fields insects or other organisms that are natural enemies of the pests that prey upon the types of plants the farmer grows. The release of these organisms reduces the population sizes of pest organisms without the use of chemicals. [*See also* AGROECOLOGY; BIODIVERSITY; FEDERAL INSECTICIDE, FUNGICIDE, AND RODENTICIDE ACT (FIFRA); FUNGICIDE; HERBICIDE; INSECTICIDE; ORGANIC FARMING; PEST CONTROL; POLLUTION; and SUSTAINABLE AGRICULTURE.]

◆ Wheat being harvested. Machines, such as this harvester, replace manpower in modern agriculture.

Agricultural Revolution

❚❭The period of human history when societal structure changed from that of a HUNTER-GATHERER SOCIETY to a society based on raising crops and LIVESTOCK. The earliest human societies lived as hunter-gatherers. In this lifestyle, people obtained the things they needed to live directly from the ENVIRONMENT by fishing or HUNTING and by gathering nuts, berries, leaves, and other food.

The hunter-gatherer lifestyle was the main societal structure until the agricultural revolution. The agricultural revolution occurred around 8000 B.C. During this period in history, people began raising crops and animals to make food

available for themselves and their families.

The agricultural revolution brought about several major changes in the ways people lived. By growing crops and raising livestock, people no longer had to move about constantly to find food. As a result, people began to establish permanent settlements and develop small farming communities. In addition, the increased food supply provided the resources needed to support an increase in the size of the human population. The availability of food also helped reduce death rates by decreasing the number of people who died from diseases related to MALNUTRITION and from starvation.

Over time, the success of agriculture as a means of meeting society's food needs allowed individuals to spend more of their time in leisure activities. It became clear that the amount of crops grown on a single farm far exceeded the

◆ The agricultural revolution resulted in the cultivation and harvesting of crops, which led to people's settling in one place instead of following a nomadic hunting-gathering lifestyle.

needs of the family living on the farm. Thus, many people began establishing towns and cities located near farms. These people developed skills in making products that could be traded with farmers for food. As population sizes in towns and cities began to increase,

◆ Today's large-scale agriculture uses technological solutions to problems. An example is the use of helicopters to spray pesticides.

◆ Agroecologists develop farming practices that do not involve synthetic pesticides and that save water and energy. These practices are used to raise crops, such as corn.

people started to have even more leisure time. To fill this time, people could spend some of their nonworking hours developing their education, establishing religions, and designing governments and laws to help the towns and cities operate more efficiently. [*See also* DEMOGRAPHY and POPULATION GROWTH.]

Agroecology

▮ The science of applying ecological principles to agriculture. Agroecologists develop farming practices that use few synthetic, or human-made, PESTICIDES and fertilizers and that conserve water and energy. Synthetic pesticides and fertilizers can harm the ENVIRONMENT. Water and energy are precious resources that must be conserved.

Agroecologists are concerned not just with protecting crops and LIVESTOCK, but also with protecting entire ECOSYSTEMS. To develop a new type of pesticide, an agroecologist might use information about natural plant chemicals from PLANTS that discourage pest attacks.

◆ Alfalfa, a crop that increases the nitrogen content of soil, provides the fertilizers needed by corn crops planted beside it.

◆ A contour-plowed field allows every furrow to receive and retain water.

To develop a new method to keep SOIL moist and fertile, an agroecologist might draw on current scientific knowledge about nutrient cycles in ecosystems. Agroecologists also employ many of the ORGANIC FARMING practices already in use, including INTEGRATED PEST MANAGEMENT, CROP ROTATION, and NO-TILL AGRICULTURE.

As the world population and its need for food continues to grow, the field of agroecology is likely to increase in importance. Its methods may replace many current agricultural techniques, which can alter and damage ecosystems. [*See also* AGROFORESTRY; PEST CONTROL; and SUSTAINABLE AGRICULTURE.]

Agroforestry

❚T̲he cultivation of trees and agricultural crops on the same land. Agroforesters plant trees, such as pecan, walnut, green ash, oak, and maple in wide rows 40–64 feet (12–19 meters) apart. Between the rows of trees, farm crops such as corn, wheat, or soybeans are grown. The growth of agricultural crops generates income during the 12–15 years needed for the trees to mature enough to produce earnings from nuts or lumber.

PLANTS other than crop plants are sometimes grown in the alleyways between trees. For example, ornamental shrubs used for landscaping may be cultivated and sold

◆ Agroforestry is a wise use of land, making it more productive while protecting the soil from erosion and providing carbon-dioxide-using, oxygen-giving organisms to help Earth.

◆ Cows graze among trees on crops such as clover and orchardgrass.

for profit. The SOIL may also be used to raise cover crops, such as clover and orchardgrass, which grazing animals eat. When fodder crops are grown under rows of walnut trees, agroforesters have noted that the yield is about 30% higher than for similiar crops grown in conventional fields.

AGROFORESTRY AND THE ENVIRONMENT

The growth of trees and agricultural crops on the same land helps reduce soil EROSION, according to a study conducted by the University of Missouri-Columbia. On highly decomposable soil, the loss may be reduced to less than 5 tons (4.5 metric tons) per 1 acre (4 square meters) per year.

Trees, like other plants, absorb CARBON DIOXIDE and give off OXYGEN. These functions may help to slow the GREENHOUSE EFFECT. Some scientists suggest that agroforestry should be used for reforestation in some areas. Such LAND USE would benefit the grower by providing profit from short-term crops. It would benefit all living things because the trees and plants absorb atmospheric carbon dioxide and convert it to plant BIOMASS. [*See also* AGROECOLOGY; FOREST PRODUCTS INDUSTRY; GLOBAL WARMING; RENEWABLE RESOURCES; and TREE FARMING.]

Air

See ATMOSPHERE

Air Pollution

▶The release of potentially harmful substances into the ATMOSPHERE. Air pollution is caused directly by primary pollutants, including the SULFUR DIOXIDE and CARBON MONOXIDE that are released during burning. These pollutants are harmful to organisms and the ENVIRONMENT. Damage to the environment can also occur from secondary pollutants, which form when primary pollutants react with other substances in the air. Examples of secondary pollutants are ACID RAIN and SMOG, the yellowish haze found in the air of big cities like New York and Los Angeles.

Most air pollution results from human activities, particularly the burning of FUELS for heat, ELECTRICITY, and use in motor vehicles. Some air pollutants come from natural sources, such as volcanoes and the breakdown of organic matter.

Since the United States began monitoring air pollution levels following the passage of the CLEAN AIR ACT in 1970, levels of some pollutants have been significantly reduced. Nevertheless, air pollution continues to cause environmental damage on both a local and a global scale. Amendments to the Clean Air Act in 1990 have placed further restrictions on the amounts of air pollutants that can be released by AUTOMOBILES and industry.

MAJOR AIR POLLUTANTS AND THEIR SOURCES

Each year, vast amounts of pollutants are poured into the atmosphere, posing health threats to humans and damaging the environment. Air is cleansed naturally by air circulation patterns and by vegetation on Earth. Today, however, this process is threatened by the increasing use of FOSSIL FUELS, expansion of industry, and the growing use of motor vehicles. The most common and widespread air pollutants produced by human activities are sulfur dioxide, NITROGEN OXIDES, carbon monoxide, HYDROCARBONS, and PARTICULATES. Some of them are direct threats to the environment and human health; others cause damage when combined with other substances in the air.

Sulfur Dioxide

Sulfur dioxide (SO_2) is a gas released when sulfur-containing fuels such as COAL and oil are burned in coal-burning power plants, paper mills, chemical plants, and PETROLEUM refineries. It is also given off by volcanoes, decaying organic matter, and OCEANS. When inhaled, it can damage the lungs and cause respiratory problems. However, it is most damaging when it combines with water droplets in the atmosphere to form acid rain. A 1992 report by the COUNCIL ON ENVIRONMENTAL QUALITY states that sulfur dioxide makes up 16% of the air pollution caused by the major air pollutants.

MAJOR AIR POLLUTANTS: SOURCES AND EFFECTS

Pollutants	Sources	Health/Environmental Effects
Sulfur dioxide	fossil fuel combustion	contributes to acid rain, which damages lakes, forests, metals, and stone monuments; may cause respiratory problems when inhaled
Nitrogen oxides	fossil fuel combustion	contributes to acid rain, smog, and the greenhouse effect; may cause lung irritation
Carbon monoxide	incomplete burning of fossil fuels by motor vehicles; industry	damages ability of body to absorb oxygen; contributes to smog formation
Hydrocarbons	incomplete burning of fossil fuels by motor vehicles	ozone and smog formation
Particulates	motor vehicles; industry; agriculture	damage to lungs and other respiratory problems

◆ Burning garbage in dumps is an illegal practice in many municipalities because of the resulting air pollution.

Nitrogen Oxides

Nitrogen oxides are nitrogen-containing gases that form when fossil fuels are burned by motor vehicles, power plants, and factories. The most common nitrogen oxides are NITROGEN DIOXIDE (NO_2) and nitrogen monoxide (NO). Like other primary pollutants, nitrogen oxides affect human health when inhaled directly. Their most damaging effects are on the environment and the global CLIMATE.

Nitrogen dioxide may be the most damaging of the nitrogen oxides. When released into the air, nitrogen dioxide mixes with water to form acid rain. It also contributes to SMOG, the yellowish haze often seen over large cities.

Nitrogen monoxide (NO) is released through the burning of fossil fuels. Nitrogen monoxide is a primary air pollutant. It is one of the GREENHOUSE GASES involved in the possible warming of Earth's atmosphere. Nitrogen oxides account for about 15% of air pollution caused by the five primary air pollutants.

Carbon Monoxide

Carbon monoxide (CO) is a colorless, odorless gas produced by the incomplete burning of fossil fuels. Carbon monoxide is the greatest contributor to air pollution. It accounts for almost half the POLLUTION caused by the five most important air pollutants. Cars, trucks, buses, and other motor vehicles are the main sources of carbon monoxide.

When inhaled, carbon monoxide interferes with the body's ability to transport OXYGEN. This can cause headaches, drowsiness, and even death. When combined with sunlight and other pollutants, such as nitrogen oxides and hydrocarbons, carbon monoxide also contributes to the formation of OZONE, the major component of smog. Ground level ozone is a poisonous gas that is harmful to the health of humans.

Hydrocarbons

Hydrocarbons are chemical compounds that contain only carbon and hydrogen. Hydrocarbon pollution is caused by the incomplete combustion of fossil fuels. The main sources of hydrocarbons are motor vehicles and power plants. FOREST FIRES and decaying organic matter are also sources. By themselves, hydrocarbons are not really a problem. However, when they react with other primary pollutants, they can form dangerous sec-

◆ Microscopic particles of ash, smoke, and dust, when inhaled, can cause respiratory problems.

◆ People living in large cities, such as Mexico City, are exposed daily to high levels of air pollution.

ondary pollutants such as ozone. According to 1992 statistics from the Council on Environmental Quality, hydrocarbons account for about 13% of all pollution caused by the five major air pollutants.

Particulates

Particulates are tiny particles of ash, smoke, and dust that are released into the air. The main sources of particulates are industry, motor vehicles, burning wood, construction, and agriculture. Particulates make up about 6% of the pollution caused by the major air pollutants. Because large particles tend to settle out of the air, they pose no significant threats to humans. However, large particles

that settle in water ECOSYSTEMS can be harmful to organisms living in those ecosystems. In addition, particles fine enough to be inhaled can get caught in the lungs and cause several respiratory problems.

Other Significant Air Pollutants

Although most pollution is caused by the five primary air pollutants, scientists are also concerned about the effects of other substances. These substances include CARBON DIOXIDE (CO_2), METHANE, and chlorofluorocarbons (CFCS).

Carbon dioxide occurs naturally in the atmosphere and plays an important role in controlling Earth's surface temperature, but whenever fossil fuels are burned for energy or when vegetation is burned to clear land, huge amounts of CO_2 are produced. Scientists fear that increased levels of CO_2 in the atmosphere can lead to a GREENHOUSE EFFECT and possibly GLOBAL WARMING.

CFCs are synthetic chemicals used as propellants in AEROSOL spray cans and as coolants in refrigerators and air conditioners. CFCs have been identified as contributors to ozone depletion and the destruction of the OZONE LAYER. They also contribute to the greenhouse effect.

Methane (CH_4) is the main ingredient of NATURAL GAS. Methane is released from rice paddies, swamps, bogs, cattle, and LANDFILLS. Scientists also believe methane contributes to the greenhouse effect.

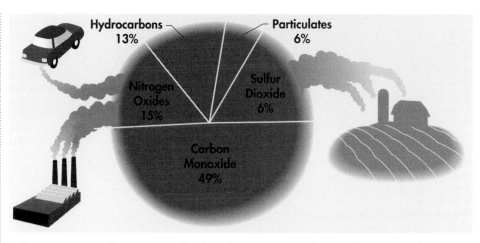

The major air pollutants are sulfur dioxide, nitrogen oxides, carbon monoxide, hydrocarbons, and particulates.

CONTROLLING AIR POLLUTION

Before 1970, the federal government established no limits on the amounts and types of pollutants that could be released into the air. Instead, concern about air pollution focused mainly on its most visible forms—the smoke, soot, and ash given off by power plants and factories. Such pollutants were controlled through voluntary cleanup efforts by industry and by state and federal programs, such as the AIR POLLUTION CONTROL ACT of 1955 and the Air Quality Act of 1967.

When the United States passed the Clean Air Act in 1970, it became the first industrialized nation to enact such sweeping laws about air pollution. Canada, Japan, Europe, and many other nations have since enacted similar laws. Under the Clean Air Act, national pollution level standards were set for six major air pollutants: carbon monoxide, LEAD (in 1977), nitrogen dioxide, ozone, sulfur dioxide, and particulates. In 1977, amendments to the Clean Air Act tightened these standards even further.

In 1990, major changes were made to the Clean Air Act. These amendments addressed four main topics: acid rain, smog, ozone depletion, and the release of toxic chemicals. To reduce the problems caused by acid rain, the act requires power plants, chemical plants, and other industries to lessen sulfur dioxide and nitrogen oxide emissions by the year 2000.

The law also sets new controls on the pollution caused by motor vehicles. The Clean Air Act of 1990 also requires industry to phase out the production and use of three chemicals that contribute to ozone depletion—CFCs, hydrochlorofluorocarbons (HCFCs), and methyl chloroform. Finally, this act forces industry to control emissions of 189 different types of toxic chemicals that pollute the air.

As a result of laws passed by the federal government since the early 1970s, pollution caused by particulates, sulfur dioxide, and lead has, to a great extent, been reduced. The use of CATALYTIC CONVERTERS on cars has further reduced carbon monoxide and hydrocarbon emissions.

The United States has also entered into several international agreements to reduce air pollution globally. For example, in 1987, 24 countries signed the MONTREAL PROTOCOL, a historic agreement to cut the production of CFCs in half by the year 2000. In 1988, 27 nations signed the United Nations Sofia Protocol, which requires reductions in nitrogen oxide emissions. [*See also* ALTERNATIVE ENERGY SOURCES; ASBESTOS; BEST AVAILABLE CONTROL TECHNOLOGY (BACT); ENERGY EFFICIENCY; OZONE HOLE; OZONE POLLUTION; SICK BUILDING SYNDROME; and ULTRAVIOLET RADIATION.]

Air Pollution Control Act (1955)

▮ The first national law in the United States designed to control AIR POLLUTION. Industrial cities were among the first to pass laws controlling factory smoke and soot. No state laws controlling air pollution existed until 1952, when Oregon became the first state to establish a major air quality control program.

The passage of the Air Pollution Control Act three years later signified that industrial air pollution had become a problem of national concern. Under this law, the federal government provided technical help and granted funds to assist states in their efforts to control air pollution at the local level. Much of the authority and power over air quality remained with the individual states until the CLEAN AIR ACT of 1970. [*See also* INDUSTRIAL REVOLUTION and LAW, ENVIRONMENTAL.]

Alaska Pipeline

▮ An oil pipeline that runs from Prudhoe Bay in northern Alaska 800 miles (1,280 kilometers) south to the port of Valdez. From Valdez, the oil is shipped in tankers to refineries on the west coast of the United States. The Alaska Pipeline is also known as the Trans-Alaskan Pipeline because it extends the entire length of the state, with the exception of the Panhandle.

A CONTROVERSY IN THE MAKING

The Alaska Pipeline has been the center of controversy since it was first proposed in 1968 after a huge deposit of oil was discovered at Prudhoe Bay. The deposit turned out to be the largest in the United States, containing about 9.6 billion barrels of oil. The companies that owned rights to the oil immediately began making plans for a pipeline to transport it to the lower 48 states.

Conservationists were worried that construction of the pipeline would harm the delicate Arctic ECO-SYSTEM it would cross. Although they filed lawsuits, delaying the project, an event occurred in 1973 that cleared the way for the pipeline.

◆ The Alaska Pipeline extends the entire length of the state, from the oil deposits at Prudhoe Bay to the port of Valdez.

◆ Oil pipelines, as well as spills from pipeline ruptures, are obstacles to the caribou's annual migration. Caribou shy away from human-made structures that cross their path.

In 1973, the Middle Eastern countries that sold oil to the United States cut off supplies. This act was in retaliation for American support of Israel during the Yom Kippur War of that year. Alarmed by the prospect of no Middle Eastern oil, Congress passed a bill in late 1973 that allowed the Alaska Pipeline to be built. By the spring of 1974, construction had begun. The first oil from Prudhoe Bay reached Valdez in July of 1977.

The construction of the pipeline was managed by the Alyeska Pipeline Service Company, a group of major oil firms, including Standard Oil, Exxon, and Phillips. More than 20,000 people were employed to construct the Alaska Pipeline. At $9 billion, it became the costliest pipeline in history, as well as the most expensive project of any kind ever attempted by private industry.

MILLIONS OF BARRELS OF OIL

The Alaska Pipeline is 48 inches (1.21 meters) in diameter and 800 miles (1,287 kilometers) long. Whereas most pipelines are buried below the surface to prevent corrosion, about half of the Alaska Pipeline is elevated above the ground. If the Alaskan Pipeline had been buried in the permafrost, heat from the oil would have melted the permafrost and caused great environmental damage.

About 1.5 million barrels of oil are transported each day through the pipeline. Pumping stations along the way keep the oil moving. When the oil reaches the port of Valdez, it is stored in tanks on top of hills. Large hoses from the storage tanks are connected to oil tankers called *supertankers*, and gravity causes the oil to flow through the hoses downward into the ships.

In 1989 one of these supertankers, the EXXON VALDEZ, caused the worst OIL SPILL in the history of the United States. The *Exxon Valdez* was loaded with about 45 million gallons (170 million liters) of oil from Prudhoe Bay when it ran into a reef in Prince William Sound, spilling about 11 million gallons (41.6 million liters) of oil into the water. The spill resulted in enormous damage to the area's marine life.

OIL UNDER A WILDLIFE REFUGE

Very close to Prudhoe Bay—about 60 miles (96 kilometers) east—is the possibility of another huge oil deposit. This deposit could contain as much as 9 billion barrels of oil, almost as much as in the Prudhoe Bay deposit. The oil could be transported easily through the Alaska Pipeline to Valdez. There is just one catch: the deposit is located under the ARCTIC NATIONAL WILDLIFE REFUGE. Because the refuge is home to a large herd of caribou and many migratory birds, the federal government has protected it from development since 1986.

After the *Exxon Valdez* disaster, public opinion was against drilling in the wildlife refuge, but the nation's need for oil may eventually override environmental concerns. If so, oil will continue to flow through the Alaska Pipeline well into the future. [*See also* OIL DRILLING.]

Algae

Plantlike organisms that live in water, SOIL, and other damp places. Algae belong to a diverse group of organisms known as **protists**. They live worldwide and are found in a great variety of shapes, sizes, and colors. Some algae SPECIES consist of only a single cell, while others, such as the seaweeds, look more like the PLANTS common to homes and gardens.

There are more than 20,000 known species of algae, making them one of the most abundant kinds of organisms. All algae contain chlorophyll, a green **pigment**

THE LANGUAGE OF THE ENVIRONMENT

coral tiny relative of jellyfish. Corals build structures called *coral reefs* by secreting chemicals from their tubelike bodies.

pigment chemical that produces color in organisms, such as the green color of plants.

protists simple organisms in the kingdom Protista, including algae, paramecia, and amoebae.

that helps plants and other organisms produce food through the process of PHOTOSYNTHESIS. Sometimes the green color of the chlorophyll is masked by other pigments, such as red, blue, purple, brown, and yellow.

As PRODUCERS, algae are important to the health of many ECOSYSTEMS. In most aquatic, or water-based, ecosystems, microscopic algae known as PHYTOPLANKTON are so numerous that they are the primary producers of nutrients. They form the critical first link in aquatic FOOD CHAINS.

Various species of algae live within the bodies and tissues of other organisms to form ecological partnerships where both species benefit. In a relationship known as SYMBIOSIS, tiny algae known as *zooxanthellae,* for example, live inside the bodies of reef-building **coral** animals. The coral obtains a steady supply of sugar from the algae. In return, the coral provides the algae with shelter and CARBON DIOXIDE.

TYPES OF ALGAE

Algae are classified into six groups. Three of these include simple, single-celled organisms, namely, the euglenoids, the diatoms, and the dinoflagellates. The remaining three groups, which usually have a multicelled structure, comprise the group called seaweeds.

Simple Algae

The euglenoids are a unique group of algae that have characteristics of both plants and animals. Best known among the euglenoids is the *Euglena,* an organism that car-

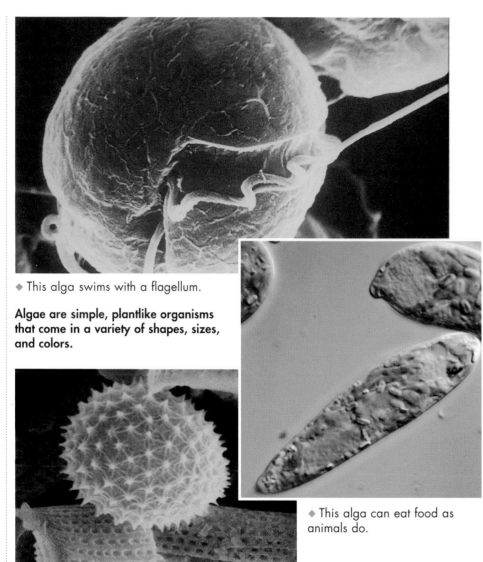

◆ This alga swims with a flagellum.

Algae are simple, plantlike organisms that come in a variety of shapes, sizes, and colors.

◆ This alga can eat food as animals do.

◆ The most abundant algae in the water are diatoms, which are also called the grass of the sea.

ries out photosynthesis but also moves around and obtains its own food when sunlight is unavailable.

The tiny diatoms, or golden algae, are a very abundant group in both freshwater and marine ecosystems. Diatoms make up a large component of phytoplankton. Most diatoms are surrounded by glass-like silica shells, with each species

having its own unique shape and design.

The dinoflagellates, another group of single-celled algae, live in all aquatic HABITATS and display a wide variety of unusual shapes and colors. Several species of dinoflagellates, such as *Gonyaulax catanella,* produce dangerous toxins, which can build up inside the

◆ The bullwhip kelps grow abundantly off the coast of Oregon.

◆ Sea lettuce are often seen on the East Coast of the United States.

◆ Red algae are typically found in tropical waters and along rocky coasts.

bodies of FISH, clams, shrimp, and other marine organisms. In warmer months, dinoflagellates sometimes reproduce rapidly, causing a reddish color in the water known as a *red tide*. During red tides, the harvesting of seafood is usually banned because of the poisons that are accumulated.

Seaweeds

The more complex algae are the seaweeds. Seaweeds, which have a clearly plantlike shape, are grouped according to their colors—green, brown, and red.

Green algae are the most diverse group of seaweeds, with approximately 7,000 species. Most green algae live in freshwater ecosystems, but some live in OCEANS. Many of the single-celled species of green algae live on the surfaces of damp soils, tree trunks, and even on the fur of a tree sloth, a slow-moving MAMMAL that lives in the RAIN FORESTS of South America.

Almost all species of brown algae are ocean dwellers that live in the cold waters of the world along rocky coasts. In contrast to green algae, there are no single-celled species of brown algae. The largest and most complex species of brown algae are the kelps, which grow in the form of thick and rubbery blades that resemble leaves. Kelps anchor themselves to rocks or the seafloor with sturdy holdfasts, which act like roots. Many species of brown algae also have air bladders. These structures help keep the algae near the surface of the water, where they can get the light they need for photosynthesis.

In many parts of the world, giant kelps grow as large as 200 feet (60 meters) in length and form vast underwater FORESTS that are home to many marine organisms. One species, *Sargassum nitans,* forms huge masses that cover the Sargasso Sea in the Atlantic Ocean.

The final seaweed group, the red algae, is a diverse one. Despite its name, it also contains brown, purple, blue, and blackish species. All species of red algae are marine organisms that are typically found in warm tropical waters and along rocky coasts. The red and blue pigments of these algae can absorb light at depths of 328 feet (100 meters) or more, allowing some species to survive on the ocean floor and in the shade of extensive kelp forests.

ALGAE AND INDUSTRY

Seaweeds are an important food source in many countries. In Japan, for example, edible seaweeds are cultivated on special farms, where thousands of tons are harvested each year. In the United States, a very useful substance, alginic acid, is obtained from kelps and other species of seaweed and used in the manufacturing of foods, such as ice cream and pudding, and in other products, such as drugs, medicinal creams, and toothpaste.

Diatomite, a substance made from the remains of diatom shells, is a useful material in industry. Containing as much as 88% silica, diatomite is used in a variety of products, such as paints, insulation materials, and abrasives. [*See also* CORAL REEF; TROPICS; and ZOO-PLANKTON.]

Algal Bloom

▶ A rapid and excessive growth of ALGAE in a pond, lake, or other freshwater ENVIRONMENT. Algal blooms often result from human activities that increase the amount of phosphorus in a pond, lake, river, or other freshwater environment. Such activities may include the discharge of DETERGENTS, SEWAGE, fertilizers, and PESTICIDES into freshwater ECOSYSTEMS. Algae and aquatic PLANTS need phosphorus to grow and carry out their life processes. If too much phosphorus enters a freshwater ecosystem, a population explosion can occur, in which the algae grow and reproduce too much. The resulting mass of algae can cover the surface of the water and clog waterways.

One of the worst effects of algal blooms occurs when large numbers of ALGAE begin to die and decay. The decay process can consume so much of the DISSOLVED OXYGEN in the water that organisms living in the water suffocate. Many algal blooms can be prevented or stopped by reducing the RUNOFF of nutrients from farmland and eliminating waste discharge into aquatic ecosystems. [*See also* BIOCHEMICAL OXYGEN DEMAND (BOD); EUTROPHICATION; and PHOSPHATES.]

◆ Wafer-thin solar cells on a flat photovoltaic solar collector. The cells contain semiconductors from which electricity flows when the semiconductors are hit by sunlight.

Alternative Energy Sources

▶ FUELS and sources of energy that are nonpolluting and renewable. Alternative energy sources are those other than the FOSSIL FUELS (COAL, oil, and NATURAL GAS) we use today. Fossil fuels are nonrenewable and cause POLLUTION.

Most economies run on fossil fuels. Fossil fuels are composed of hydrogen and CARBON; thus, they are often referred to as HYDROCARBONS. When hydrocarbons are burned, they release into the air vast amounts of CARBON DIOXIDE and other air **pollutants**. As a result of the polluting effects of these gases on the ATMOSPHERE, many people are developing alternative sources of energy to provide their power.

Some of the new technologies to develop renewable and nonpolluting alternative sources of energy are COGENERATION; SOLAR ENERGY; WIND POWER; GEOTHERMAL ENERGY; OCEAN THERMAL ENERGY CONVERSION (OTEC); and HYDROELECTRIC POWER.

COGENERATION

Americans throw out about 4 billion tons of SOLID WASTE (GARBAGE that is not a liquid or gas) annually. As LANDFILL space dwindles, governments and industries are increasingly using some of this waste material as fuel. For example, in Hawaii power plants burn sugar cane waste to generate ELECTRICITY. Using solid waste to generate energy is called *cogeneration*.

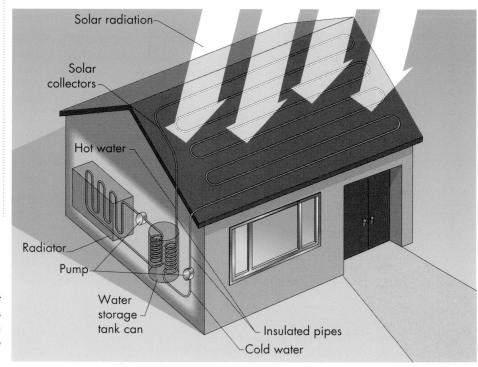

Solar radiation

Solar collectors

Hot water

Radiator

Pump

Water storage tank can

Insulated pipes

Cold water

SOLAR ENERGY

The heat produced by sunlight is a free and endless source of energy. Some solar energy systems are "passive": they use materials that are heated by sunlight and systems that channel this heat to where it is needed. For example, some houses have passive solar hot water systems. In these systems, water is heated by the sun as it flows through black piping. The heat from the water is then given off to the rooms of the house.

Much research is being done on "active" solar energy systems, particularly photovoltaic (PV) systems. As its name suggests, these systems use sunlight (photo) to create electricity (voltaic). PV systems use PHOTOVOLTAIC CELLS in which the energy contained in sunlight activates electrons in silicon semiconductors. The electricity

◆ Many different systems, such as these solar panels, have been designed to capture solar energy.

◆ The heat produced by sunlight is being captured by this solar receiver.

produced is channeled through wires to power appliances, furnaces, and other household appliances. PV technology was first developed by NASA (National Aeronautics and Space Administration) to power satellites. In the United States today, large areas of the southwestern desert are covered with PV solar panels that produce enough electricity for a small city. Some individual homes also have PV panels on the roof to provide electricity. PV panels are even mounted on solar-powered cars and send a constant current to a battery that runs the vehicle.

◆ In windy parts of the United States, windmills are used to generate electricity.

WIND POWER

In some parts of the United States where conditions are favorable, many windmills of modern design cover the landscape. The windmill rotors turn and produce electricity in generators. Windmill "farms" can also provide enough electricity for small cities. As the technology advances, wind may prove to be the most efficient alternative energy source: the windiest places on the planet could produce ten times the electricity now used worldwide!

GEOTHERMAL ENERGY

Geothermal electricity is produced when water is heated by hot rocks below Earth's surface. In Iceland, lava and intensely hot water flow just under the surface of the land. This energy has been harnessed and used to keep Icelanders' homes snug and warm all winter. New technologies are being developed to harness the heat and energy in volcanoes and superheated subsurface materials to heat homes and run generators that produce electricity.

OCEAN THERMAL ENERGY

Scientists are looking for ways to use the immense power of the ocean waves, or **tides,** and temperature variations at different depths to produce electricity without harming the marine ECOSYSTEM. For example, the movement of coastal tides through a turbine could create huge amounts of electricity. Yet building a plant that could accomplish this would likely destroy coastal and marine fisheries and shellfisheries, because these organisms depend on the movement of the tides for their survival. It will probably take some time before environmentally safe technologies of this sort are perfected.

HYDROGEN

Water has two atoms of hydrogen and one of oxygen (H_2O). The oceans contain an unimaginable amount of hydrogen. Technologies are being developed in which hydrogen derived from water can be used as a fuel and a source of energy. To remove the hydrogen from water, an electric current is passed through the water in a process known as *hydrolysis*. Large amounts of electricity are needed in this process, making it an expensive way to produce electricity. Some critics of hydrogen technology fear that this gas is too flammable for everyday use. Its supporters continue to improve the process of making this abundant fuel.

Aluminum

▶ A lightweight, silvery, corrosion-resistant, easily bendable metal. These properties make aluminum highly useful and ideal for making containers for drinks and foods, as well as building material. Because aluminum occurs naturally only in combination with other MINERALS, it is expensive to mine and extract. Bauxite, its most common ore, is found mainly in tropical RAIN FOREST areas.

Aluminum cans can be melted down and used again. This process uses less than 5% of the energy needed to produce new aluminum from ore. Thus, aluminum recycling saves money and energy, as well as protects rain forest HABITATS.

Metallic aluminum is relatively safe; however, aluminum in compounds can be dissolved by ACID RAIN, allowing aluminum to enter the SOIL and groundwater, where it can become a danger to terrestrial and aquatic WILDLIFE. [*See also* MINING; RECYCLING, REDUCING, REUSING; STRIP MINING; and SURFACE MINING.]

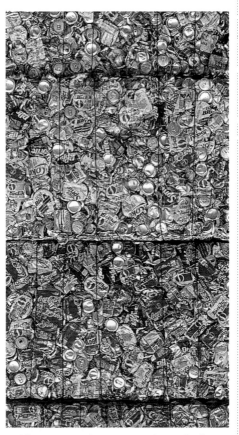

◆ Aluminum soda cans can be melted down and used again. This process uses up much less energy than it takes to make the metal from ore.

Amphibian

▶ A VERTEBRATE animal with a larval and adult stage that are distinctly different. Amphibians are often mistakenly defined as animals that spend part of their life in the water and part on land, but that is not true of all amphibians. The word *amphibian* means "two lives." The phrase refers to the very different forms that all amphibians have during their young, or larval, stage and their adult stage. All amphibians share the trait of having skin that allows water to pass through, though some have more water resistant skin than others. Since they can lose moisture through their skin, most amphibians live in moist places.

AMPHIBIAN GROUPS

Amphibians include salamanders (a group that includes newts and sirens), frogs (a group that includes toads), and a group of tropical animals called *caecilians* (wormlike, limbless amphibians that are blind). Frogs are amphibians that have four legs and no tails as adults. Biologists also call them *Anurans*. Toads are one of the groups of frogs. In North America, most toads have rough, warty skin and live on land, but some toads in other parts of the world have smooth skin, and some live in water as adults. The one reliable difference between toads and all other frogs is that toads do not have teeth, while all other groups of frogs have teeth. There are about 3,500 known species of frogs in the world, though

◆ The western toad lives in western North America.

◆ The golden toad of Central America is one of many frog species that have suddenly declined in number since the mid-1980s. Only the males have a bright orange color.

researchers think that there are more SPECIES still to be discovered in the tropics. Frogs range in size from tiny tree frogs that could easily sit on a dime to large species that weigh several pounds.

Salamanders are amphibians that have tails and legs as adults. Most species have four legs as adults, though some have only two. There are salamanders that measure only about 1 inch (2.5 centimeters) long as adults. Two species that live in Asia—the giant Japanese salamander and the giant Chinese salamander—can grow up to lengths of about 5.5 feet (about 1.7 meters). There are about 350 species of salamanders in the world. Newts are salamanders that live in water as air-breathing adults, and often spend a portion of their lives as terrestrial animals, in between being aquatic larvae and aquatic adults. Sirens are salamanders that stay in water their whole lives, and never lose their gills.

The final group of amphibians are the legless, burrowing animals called *caecilians*. Some live on land; others live entirely in the water. The largest caecilians can reach lengths of about 4 feet (1.2 meters), but the smallest are only about 2.5 inches (6.5 centimeters) when fully grown. All 130 species of caecilians live in the TROPICS.

REPRODUCTION OF AMPHIBIANS

All amphibians begin their lives as eggs. Unlike BIRD or REPTILE eggs, amphibian eggs do not have a waterproof outer shell and must incubate in a moist place. Most, but not all, amphibians lay their eggs in water. Some salamanders lay their eggs under moist rotting logs in FORESTS. Some frog species lay their eggs in foamy masses attached to branches and leaves that hang over streams; others carry masses of eggs on their backs. The Surinam

toad of South America carries its eggs in pockets on the back of the female until the young toads emerge. The gastric brooding frog of Australia actually swallows its tadpoles, allowing them to develop in its stomach. While the young are inside, the adult does not eat and produces no digestive fluids.

Larval amphibians are little more than swimming digestive systems. Larval frogs are called *tadpoles*, but there is no special word for larval salamanders or caecilians. In most amphibians, the larva lives in water and feeds until it gains enough mass and energy to change, or **metamorphose**, into an adult.

The metamorphosis of the tadpole into a frog is an amazing process. An aquatic creature with gills, a tail, and no legs changes, sometimes in only a matter of days, into an adult with legs and lungs. Some salamander adults do not have lungs. They take in oxygen directly through their skin. Other salamanders retain their gills even as adults. Some amphibians, such as the common bullfrog, can stay

The red-backed salamander is common in the northeastern United States. It is an amphibian but does not breed in water. It lays its eggs under moist logs in the forest.

THE LANGUAGE OF THE ENVIRONMENT

metamorphose to change. Animals that metamorphose undergo a dramatic change in body shape at some time in their lives, such as a tadpole becoming a frog or a caterpillar becoming a butterfly.

in the larval stage for several years. Others, such as the spadefoot toad of the American desert, grow from egg to larva to adult in only a few weeks.

Unlike any other vertebrate group, all adult amphibians are CARNIVORES. They eat INSECTS, small animals, and small FISH. Many of the young are carnivores, but some larvae are HERBIVORES, eating only plants, or OMNIVORES, eating both plants and animals.

IMPORTANT LINKS IN THE FOOD CHAIN

It was once thought that amphibians were of little importance to their ECOSYSTEMS, but that view is changing. For example, the most common amphibian in the northeastern United States is the red-backed salamander, found under logs and leaves in almost every forest in the region. One study in New Hampshire found that red-backed salamanders produced as much BIOMASS in some types of forest each year as all of the bird species in that type of forest combined, and about five times as much biomass as all of the small MAMMAL species put together! Red-backed salamanders are small but numerous. These salamanders are an important link in the FOOD CHAIN. They feed between the tiny forest INVERTEBRATES they eat and larger PREDATORS. Throughout the world, amphibians are important as predators of invertebrates and as prey for other species.

WARNINGS FROM AMPHIBIANS

Because they have water-permeable skin and breed mostly in WETLANDS, amphibians make excellent indicators of environmental problems. For example, in the early 1970s, a researcher at Cornell University noticed that the eggs of local populations of yellow-spotted salamanders were dying in the temporary ponds where they breed. On investigating, he found that the salamanders were dying of ALUMINUM poisoning. The high level of aluminum in the ponds turned out to be due to acidic rainwater that dissolved the aluminum out of the SOIL and carried it into the ponds. This was one of the first examples of damage to the ENVIRONMENT by ACID RAIN.

Since the mid-1980s, researchers who study amphibians have noticed a frightening trend in many species. Frog populations all over the world are in decline, and some species, such as the golden toad of Central America, went from being common to extinct in just a few years. The gastric brooding frog has not been seen in the wild since 1990, even in places where it was once common. Most of the disappearing frog species live at high altitudes in mountain forests. Researchers suspect that increased levels of ultraviolet light, caused by OZONE depletion, are destroying these frog populations. In 1993, researchers in the Pacific Northwest of the United States proved that high levels of ultraviolet light were killing the eggs of some species of frogs in that region.

Many researchers believe that monitoring amphibian populations is important for the protection of salamanders, frogs, and other amphibians. Such monitoring also serves human interests because amphibians, through their sensitivity to environmental change, are good indicators of environmental conditions.

Anaerobic

◗ Living or occuring in the absence of OXYGEN. Most of Earth's oxygen is produced as a by-product of the PHOTOSYNTHESIS carried out by PLANTS and ALGAE. Oxygen is present in Earth's ATMOSPHERE, in OCEAN water, or fresh water; or in compounds that make up much of the matter of Earth.

ENVIRONMENTS that are not in direct contact with the atmosphere often contain little oxygen. Such environments may include the muddy bottoms of OCEANS, ponds, lakes, and streams, the SLUDGE in SEWAGE TREATMENT PLANTS, the SOIL of LANDFILLS, and the tissues and organs (such as intestines) of other organisms. Although these environments lack oxygen, organisms called *anaerobes* have adapted to survival in such environments.

◆ The Meanders-Bolinas lagoon in California is an anaerobic environment.

◆ The soil on this mudflat along the estuary contains little or no oxygen; therefore, only certain organisms can live here.

Anaerobic organisms include some species of BACTERIA and FUNGI.

Most organisms use oxygen in the atmosphere or oxygen dissolved in water to carry out RESPIRATION. In this process, oxygen is chemically combined with food to produce energy, CARBON DIOXIDE, and water. In contrast, anaerobes do not need oxygen to extract energy from their food during RESPIRATION. One type of anaerobic respiration is alcoholic fermentation. This process produces ethanol, a type of alcohol, as a by-product. [*See also* ADAPTATION and AEROBIC.]

Ancient Forest

See OLD-GROWTH FOREST

Animal Rights

▶ **A**n active movement whose members believe that certain animals have the same rights as humans. Members of animal-rights organizations protest the HUNTING of, relocation of, and experimentation on animals.

In contrast to animal-rights activists, many scientists believe that experiments on animals are necessary to solve human health problems. In tests on animals with biological systems similar to humans, new medicines and techniques can be tried without endangering human life. Most animal-rights activists argue that animals' lives are as important as human lives. These people believe scientists should make use of research techniques such as experimenting on BACTERIA or bits of animal tissue or working on computer models rather than using animals. Because of activists' efforts, several states now require public schools to offer alternatives, such as computer programs, to dissection activities in biology classes.

Many people believe animal experimentation is worthwhile. They also believe stronger laws are needed to prevent cruelty to lab animals. Scientists insist they always treat animals humanely. They claim that such treatment is an important part of their research, since any pain or suffering felt by an animal during experimentation could result in undependable research data. Scientists add that

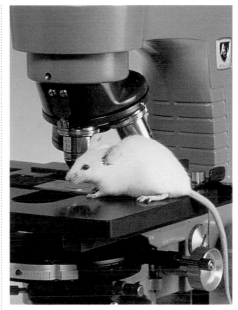

◆ Advocates for animal rights are against the use of animals in tests, such as those done by cosmetic and drug makers.

alternative techniques are not always appropriate. When a new drug is tested, for example, knowledge of how it affects a few bits of tissue cannot reveal how it might affect an entire body.

LAWS AND PROTESTS

Although the Animal Welfare Act of 1966 requires scientists working in the United States to furnish satisfactory food and shelter for some lab animals, it does not limit the kinds of experiments that can be done. Some limits are set by government or private organizations that provide funding for the research projects. Laws in 14 states prohibit the release of animals from a pound to a research lab. However, eight other states require pounds to release animals to labs.

Animal-rights organizations protest the killing of wild animals to provide fur coats for the fashion industry. Members not only give speeches and write letters objecting to the wearing of fur; they also picket fur salons and have even sprayed paint on fur coats worn by people. Such protests have had an impact on the fur industry. Today it is more fashionable for women to wear faux, or synthetic, fur coats.

SAVING A SINGLE ANIMAL

Activists also protest the treatment of an individual animal if they believe its rights are being violated. For example, members of the Progressive Animal Welfare Society (PAWS) of Seattle, Washington, recently rallied to save Ivan, a 32-year-old, 400-pound (180-kilogram) silverback GORILLA. Captured as an infant in Zaire, Ivan lived in a 40-by-40-foot (12-by-12-meter) cage inside a shopping center, where he was used as a tourist attraction. He had never been allowed outdoors. PAWS members staged protests, wrote petitions, and investigated the possibility of a lawsuit to force owners of the shopping center to stop the inhumane treatment of the gorilla. The organization was successful: the shopping center closed down, and Zoo Atlanta agreed to take Ivan. At the zoo, Ivan was first placed in a cage, then gradually released to the outdoors, where he is now able to walk on real grass for the first time in 26 years. [*See also* ENDANGERED SPECIES and WILDLIFE CONSERVATION.]

Antarctica

▶ Earth's southernmost continent, which lies in an area surrounding the South Pole. The continent occupies an area about 1.5 times larger in size than the continental United States. Nearly all of Antarctica is always covered by a sheet of ice that is about 1.25 miles (2 kilometers) thick. Unlike the ARCTIC, Antarctica is a continent because it rests on base rock. At least 80% of the world's fresh water is locked up in the Antarctic ice sheet. If this vast ice sheet melted, scientists estimate, Earth's sea level would rise about 200 feet (61 meters) worldwide.

One might think that with all this frozen water, Antarctica is a wet place. However, it receives less than 4 to 6 inches (10 to 15 centimeters) of PRECIPITATION each year. For this reason, Antarctica is actually a DESERT—a cold desert. The blizzards that rage across the continent blow around snow, but very little precipitation falls.

Because it is located in the Southern Hemisphere, the seasons of Antarctica are opposite those of the United States and other countries in the Northern Hemisphere. During the winter months the sun never rises, so night lasts 24 hours each day. Because of Earth's tilt and movement around the sun, Antarctica and the Arctic region in the North Pole are pointed away from the sun throughout their winter months. Likewise, because the sun never sets during the summer months, this time of year has 24 hours of daylight. Even with all this

sunshine, temperatures rarely rise above freezing or 32° F (0° C). The coldest temperature recorded was −128° F (−89° C).

Animals that live in Antarctica are well adapted to their ENVIRONMENT. During summers, penguins lie flat on the snow to cool themselves. If temperatures rise above freezing, the penguins pant to give up heat from their bodies. Other animals of Antarctica, such as seals, are insulated from the cold by the **blubber** on their bodies. The penguins and seals feed on the large amounts of FISH living in the waters off Antarctica.

Near the bottom of the Antarctic FOOD CHAIN are shrimplike krill. These tiny animals are the main food of baleen WHALES. Orcas,

or killer whales, feed on seals. Until the threat of whale EXTINCTION encouraged many nations to stop whaling, whales were the most sought-after resource in Antarctica. Antarctica is also an important nesting area for many SPECIES of migrating BIRDS.

By 1943, Argentina, Chile, Australia, Norway, France, New Zealand, and Great Britain claimed ownership of parts of Antarctica. These countries based their claims

THE LANGUAGE OF THE ENVIRONMENT

blubber the layer of fat beneath the skin of whales and other large marine mammals.

preserve a place where wild animals are managed and protected.

◆ Penguins, seals, and whales are among the larger animals that make their home in Antarctica. In the ocean surrounding this continent, small shrimplike animals called krill exist in great numbers.

Antarctic Treaty

◆ Antarctica is the world's southernmost continent. At least 80% of the world's fresh water is located up in the Antarctic ice sheet.

◗**A**n agreement, originally signed on December 1, 1959, by 12 nations with interests in ANTARCTICA, encouraging cooperation of nations and assuring peaceful scientific investigation on the continent. The treaty nations include Argentina, Australia, Belgium, Chile, France, Great Britain, Japan, New Zealand, Norway, the former Soviet Union, South Africa, and the United States.

on their nearness to the continent or to exploration of it by their peoples. In the 1970s, these countries, along with the United States, Japan, the former Soviet Union, South Africa, and Belgium, signed the ANTARCTIC TREATY to help preserve Antarctica. The treaty permits member nations to do scientific research and carry out other peaceful activities on the continent. The treaty discourages countries from removing Antarctica's resources, and it tries to prevent economic use of the continent. Preservationists and concerned scientists are working to get treaty nations to ban all depletion of Antarctic resources. They would like Antarctica to be classified as a "world wildlife **preserve**," to be saved for future generations. [*See also* BIOME; INTERNATIONAL CONVENTION FOR THE REGULATION OF WHALING (ICRW); INTERNATIONAL WHALING COMMISSION (IWC); and TUNDRA.]

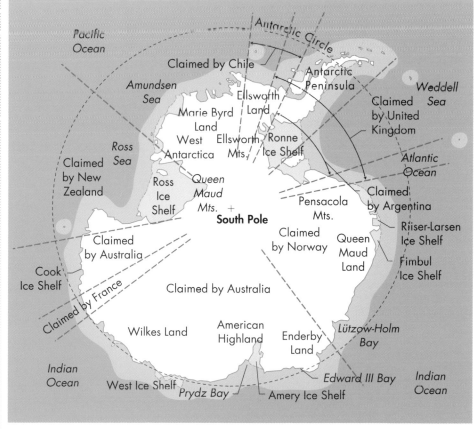

◆ In the 1970s, several countries signed the Antarctic Treaty to preserve Antarctica.

Although the 30-year treaty neither accepted nor rejected any nation's territorial claims, it set aside the area below 60°S latitude for scientific research by all. The treaty also banned military operations and large-scale MINING on Antarctica. To enforce the ban on mining, the treaty allows for mutual inspection of sites and routine exchange of data on current scientific activities.

In 1988, a new treaty was introduced that would permit controlled oil and MINERAL exploration on Antarctica. Some scientists believe these kinds of activities could have serious consequences for local and world ENVIRONMENTS because of Antarctica's delicately balanced ECOSYSTEM. The continent has no land PLANTS but has abundant sea life, which could be threatened by oil and mineral exploration of the area. For example, in 1989, an OIL SPILL from a tanker off Antarctica killed thousands of penguins and skuas. [*See also* OIL DRILLING.]

Aquaculture

▌The raising of FISH, or other aquatic animals or PLANTS, in artificial ENVIRONMENTS. Aquaculture involves creating an environment that contains all of the necessary materials needed for raising or "growing" aquatic animals and plants that humans use for food. Aquaculture facilities may include human-made ponds or pools that

◆ Agriculturists create an environment to "grow" aquatic animals and plants that can be used as human food.

◆ In China, freshwater fish are raised in artificial ponds.

have either fresh water or salt water. The nutrients needed by the growing animals or plants, the water temperature, and the OXYGEN content of the water are also controlled. In addition, HABITAT features, such as surfaces to which shellfish can attach as they grow, may be provided.

Aquaculture began in China about 4,000 years ago. The Chinese developed aquaculture by raising freshwater fish in artificial ponds. Today, China continues to be the world leader in aquaculture.

One kind of aquaculture is called *fish farming*. Fish farming involves the creation of a series of ponds, each stocked with a SPECIES of fish at a particular stage of development. Clean water is circulated through the ponds. As it circulates, the water brings needed oxygen to the pond and removes wastes. When the fish are mature, they are harvested. The harvested fish may be sent to markets alive or they may be killed and shipped. In the United States, most of the catfish, crayfish, and rainbow trout, and about one-half the shellfish consumed by people, are produced by fish farms.

Ranch farming is a kind of aquaculture in which young fish are raised in an artificial environment until they reach adult age. The fish are then set free. SALMON are often raised this way. Though young salmon develop in fresh water, adults live most of their lives in salt water. Salmon ranchers release mature salmon into streams. The salmon swim to the ocean, where they live for several years. When they are ready to mate, the adult salmon return to the freshwa-ter habitat where they were born. The adult salmon then spawn in their ranch habitat. Following spawning, the adult salmon are killed and sent to markets. The eggs laid by the salmon develop and grow into young salmon in the ranch environment until they are mature enough for release into streams.

There is an environmental downside to aquaculture. Fish grown through aquaculture are raised in extremely crowded conditions. Fish wastes sometimes create a WATER POLLUTION problem. In addition, aquacultural operations require enormous amounts of water. Despite these individual problems, most aquaculture does not seriously harm the environment. In fact, aquaculture will likely continue to provide a needed source of food for a constantly increasing human population. [*See also* DAMS; FISH LADDER; FISHING, COMMERCIAL; and FISHING, RECREATIONAL.]

Aquifer

An underground region where SOIL or porous rock contains water. Some aquifers are confined—they are areas of water-saturated rock trapped between top and bottom layers of rock that water cannot pass through. Others are unconfined, which means there is no layer of water-impermeable rock on top of the aquifer. The water in aquifers slowly filters down the slope of whatever impermeable layer it rests on. Water from aquifers can emerge into the open as **springs**, or filter into rivers, lakes, or the ocean. Water in aquifers can also be brought to the surface with **wells**.

Rainwater that falls to Earth may be absorbed by soil and stored in spaces between rocks and soil particles. This fresh water that collects underground is called *groundwater*. Groundwater that collects in spaces formed by rocks is stored in aquifers.

AQUIFER FORMATION

About one-third of all the water that falls on land percolates down into the soil and rocks to become part of an aquifer. Some of the spaces in the rock layers contain

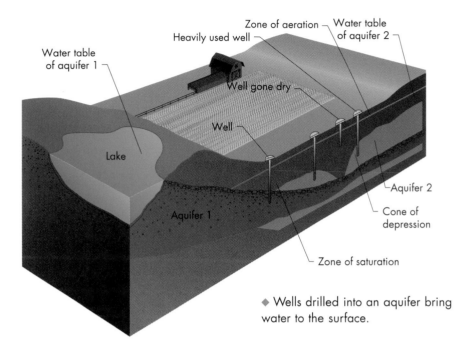

Wells drilled into an aquifer bring water to the surface.

water, while others contain air. Beneath the rock spaces filled with air is a rock layer in which all spaces are filled with water. This water-filled layer is called the ZONE OF SATURATION. The upper surface of the zone of saturation forms the WATER TABLE. The higher the water table, the easier it is to pump water to the surface. Water at the bottom of an aquifer is under pressure. This water will move naturally toward an area of lower pressure such as a spring, which provides an outlet to the surface.

The place where an aquifer fills is called the *recharge area*. Often, this area lies hundreds of miles from the main aquifer. For instance, in the United States, the Floridian Aquifer lies beneath southern Georgia and northern Florida. This aquifer is recharged by rain that falls in the hills of western Georgia and eastern Alabama.

The Ogallala Aquifer is the largest aquifer in the world. It lies under the Great Plains region of the United States.

Aquifers are usually made up of porous rocks, such as sandstone and gravel, that have many air spaces in which water can accumulate. Occasionally, aquifers contain large areas of water that do not have any rocks. For example, limestone may dissolve to form caves that fill with water.

THE IMPORTANCE OF AQUIFERS

In most parts of the world, including the dry deserts of Saudi Arabia and the drier areas of the western United States, people rely on aquifers to meet their water needs. The groundwater contained in aquifers is used in industry, for crop IRRIGATION, and in the home. The largest aquifer in the world is the Ogallala Aquifer, located in the central United States. This aquifer supplies most of the water used by people living in the states making up the big plains region of the United States.

PROBLEMS INVOLVED WITH USING AQUIFERS FOR WATER

Using groundwater to meet the needs of an area is not without problems. Economics is one concern of obtaining water from aquifers. Economics deals mostly with the cost of building the wells that pump water to the surface. Building and maintaining these wells can be very expensive.

In most aquifers, water moves only about 3 to 6 feet (1 to 2 meters) per day. Therefore, it may take hundreds of years to replace water that is pumped out of an

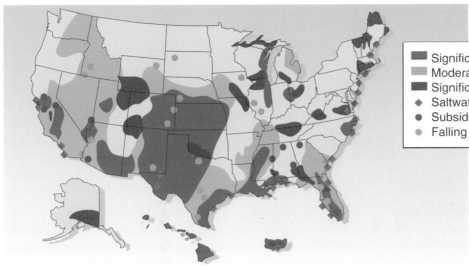

■ Significant ground water overdraft
■ Moderate ground water overdraft
■ Significant ground water pollution
◆ Saltwater intrusion
● Subsidence
● Falling water levels in springs and streams

aquifer. Poor management of wells and aquifers can lead to problems, such as water depletion and the formation of sinkholes, POLLUTION, and SALTWATER INTRUSION.

Depletion and the Formation of Sinkholes

A depression forms in the water table around a well. This depression may eventually reach the part of the well that takes in water. When this happens, the well runs dry and the water source is depleted.

When a well runs dry, the ground above an aquifer may sink and collapse because it now contains air instead of water. Such conditions have caused the sinkholes that have developed in several southern states in the United States in recent years. Venice, a city on the coast of Italy, has subsided, or sunken, gradually from aquifer depletion. In fact, Venice has subsided more than 9 feet (3 meters) since it was founded 1,500 years ago. San Jose, California, has sunk 9 feet (3 meters) over the last 50 years due to depletion of an aquifer.

Pollution

Until the 1970s, groundwater pollution was thought to be caused by substances that pollute surface water by the ground above it. We now know that groundwater can be contaminated in many ways.

Groundwater from sandy rock is often very clean because sand has large surface areas upon which impurities are absorbed. This cleansing process works particularly well for biological impurities, such as BACTERIA, that stick to the sand grains and then act as DECOMPOSERS to break down organic matter in the water.

In contrast, many chemical pollutants, such as industrial wastes and PESTICIDES, are not removed by filtration through sand. Chemical pollutants pose even greater problems for aquifers that are not made of sandy material. For example, aquifers in Florida contain large amounts of limestone. More than 1,000 wells have been shut down because of contamination with a PESTICIDE used to kill roundworms. The cleanup following Hurricane Andrew in 1992 made aquifer pollution problems in Florida even worse. After the hurricane, military and local people set fire to piles of waste. TOXIC WASTES and pollutants contained in the remaining ashes were washed into the aquifer by rainwater.

How severe is the aquifer pollution problem? Water scientists in California estimate that pollutants in one-fifth of the state's drinking water wells exceed state pollution limits. Industrial solvents and gasoline from leaks at gas stations are the most common pollutants, especially around Los Angeles and San Francisco. In Iowa, other chemicals threaten the water supply. Pesticides and other synthetic chemicals, many from fertilizers, have been detected in more than half of the city wells in Iowa.

Saltwater Intrusion

Salt water seeps into the many depleted aquifers located near coastlines. Fresh water is less dense than salt water. As a result, fresh water from rainfall lies on top of salt

Aquifer ◆ 37

water that percolates into aquifers from the sea. The density difference between fresh water and salt water is such that a balanced state develops in which fresh water extends about 128 feet (40 meters) below sea level for every 3 feet (1 meter) that the water table on land extends above sea level. Thus, if the freshwater table is lowered by only 6 feet (2 meters), the salt water beneath the fresh water will rise as much as 256 feet (78 meters). This salt water may contaminate wells and irrigation systems. In the western part of Long Island, New York, so much groundwater was pumped out of an aquifer that the salt water level rose and contaminated the wells. Today, water for this area has to be supplied by pipes from the mainland.

AQUIFER RESTORATION

The restoration of a polluted or depleted aquifer is a long-term process. First, pollution must be stopped from entering the aquifer. Then, ways must be found to recharge the aquifer with clean fresh water. There is no short-term way to remove hazardous pollutants from an aquifer. If additional pollution of an aquifer is prevented, an aquifer will eventually cleanse itself. This process occurs as polluted water is slowly replaced by clean water that enters the aquifer at the recharge area.

In some places, attempts have been made to recharge aquifers artificially by pumping clean water down into them. However, the usual method for recharging an aquifer is to limit the amount of water removed and permit the aquifer to recharge naturally. Venice, Italy, attempted to recharge the aquifer located beneath the city, partly by rationing the withdrawal of water. As a result of these efforts, the subsiding of the city has also slowed. [*See also* ARTESIAN WELL; CONSERVATION; and WATER, DRINKING.]

Arctic

▶The region lying north of the Arctic Circle and surrounding the North Pole. The Arctic Circle is sometimes defined as the northern limit above which trees typically will not grow.

The area known as the Arctic is made up mostly of pack ice formed from the waters of the Arctic Ocean. In addition, some small islands and parts of North America, Europe, and Asia are located in the Arctic. Because it rests mostly on ocean rather than land, the Arctic is not a continent.

During much of the year, most of the Arctic is made up of large sheets of ice. This ice melts somewhat during the summer months, allowing the Arctic to become more like an OCEAN than a mass of ice. When the temperature of the sea water falls below 28° F (–3° C), the water refreezes to form pack ice. In winter, the pack ice may form a mass greater than 2,500 square miles (6,250 square kilometers) across and several feet thick that floats atop the ocean. These massive ice sheets collide and form pressure ridges as ice sheets slide over one another.

ARCTIC SEASONS

Nightlike darkness marks the winter months in the Arctic 24 hours a day. These conditions result from the tilt of Earth's axis. During summer months, daylight lasts for 24 hours each day. During this period of total daylight, temperatures may rise to 60° F (16° C). These balmy temperatures allow for a short growing season that supports various tundra PLANTS and animals, such as INSECTS and migrating BIRDS.

The climate of the Arctic is harsh. Winter temperatures in the Arctic are typically about –60° F (–51° C). Despite these low temperatures, the Arctic does support a variety of WILDLIFE.

ARCTIC WILDLIFE

In the northernmost sections of the Arctic, typical animals include polar bears, SEALS AND SEA LIONS, and walruses. Farther south, where the Arctic becomes TUNDRA, animal life becomes more diverse. This land supports arctic hares, ptarmigans, ermines, and arctic foxes and wolves.

In the tundra region of the Artic, the land consists of a SOIL layer called *permafrost*. Permafrost is a soil layer that remains completely frozen throughout the year. Above the permafrost layer, a thin layer of soil may thaw enough to support the growth of plants during warmer spring and summer months. Because of the layer of permafrost below the upper soil layer, water that falls in the tundra during spring and summer cannot drain deep into the soil. Thus, water may collect on the surface of the land to form bogs. The bogs provide HABITAT for a variety of insects. Migrating birds that feed upon the insects are common in bog areas.

Some flowering plants, such as poppies, bluebells, and grasses, grow in the tundra during warmer months. LICHENS are also common. The lichens and plants support populations of migrating animals such as muskoxen and caribou. Although the Arctic is sometimes described as treeless, some trees, such as the birch, do grow in the tundra region of the Arctic. Unlike the birch that grow in DECIDUOUS FORESTS, the birch and other trees of the tundra are of dwarf varieties. The dwarf size of these trees is an ADAPTATION that helps prevent water loss and damage caused by harsh winds. [*See also* ANTARCTICA; ARCTIC NATIONAL WILDLIFE REFUGE (ANWR); BIOME; and TAIGA.]

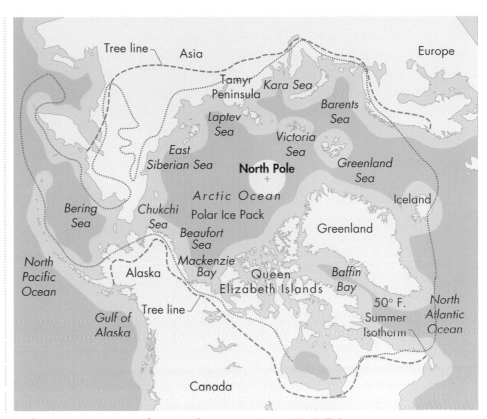

◆ The Arctic is an ice-pack region that surrounds the North Pole.

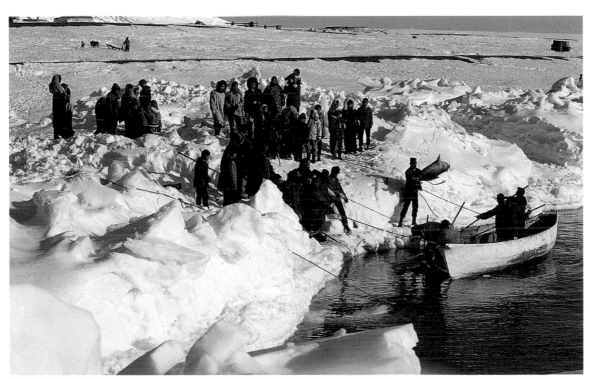

◆ Inuit villagers watch while hunters dissect a whale. Afterwards, the whale is divided among them.

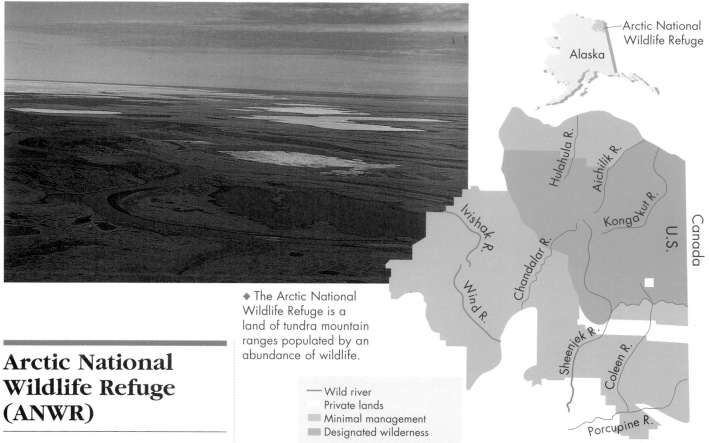

◆ The Arctic National Wildlife Refuge is a land of tundra mountain ranges populated by an abundance of wildlife.

— Wild river
　 Private lands
　 Minimal management
　 Designated wilderness

Arctic National Wildlife Refuge (ANWR)

▶A 1.5-million-acre (0.6 million hectare) WILDERNESS preserve and vital refuge for caribou and migrating shore BIRDS in northeastern Alaska near the oil fields of Prudhoe Bay. Geologists working for oil companies believe there might be PETROLEUM deposits off the shore of ANWR (commonly pronounced an-wahr). Its nearness to the developed oil fields in Prudhoe Bay would make extracting oil from ANWR cost-effective for these oil companies. Supporters of drilling for oil off the coast of ANWR point out that the United States is too dependent on oil imported from foreign countries.

People against opening the WILDLIFE refuge to oil exploration

◆ The area near Lake Schrader in ANWR is a designated wilderness area.

◆ Caribou and oxen are part of the Arctic ecosystem. Many species of migratory shore birds have nesting sites here.

insist that the last great herd of caribou in North America will lose its crucial calving and feeding grounds if oil development intrudes on the refuge. The severe disruption of irreplaceable nesting sites for migratory shore birds (which fly from all over the world to the high ARCTIC to nest) might even cause their populations to decline.

Arctic Alaska is TUNDRA—a BIOME in which the SOIL just beneath the surface is permanently frozen. Experience has shown that spilled oil will stay on the surface of tundra because it cannot sink beneath the frozen permafrost. Ponds of surface oil poison any PLANTS and animals that come into contact with them. Once this fragile ENVIRONMENT is degraded, there is little likelihood that it can ever be restored.

Scientists put forward an economic argument for maintaining the refuge in ANWR. Even if the maximum amount of oil projected by oil company geologists is found at ANWR, this amount will fuel only a small fraction of our economy for less than one year.

Congress determines what can or cannot be done in a NATIONAL WILDLIFE REFUGE. For years, a congressional battle raged over whether or not to open ANWR to oil exploration. The devastating 1989 OIL SPILL by the EXXON VALDEZ in Prince William Sound in southern Alaska convinced enough members of Congress to pass legislation that, for a while, spared ANWR from the environmental impacts of OIL DRILLING. [See also ALASKA PIPELINE; OIL POLLUTION; PETROLEUM; and WILDLIFE CONSERVATION.]

Army Corps of Engineers

▶ A unit of the U.S. Army responsible for the construction of many water management projects. In the United States, the Flood Control Act of 1938 provided federal money for waterway projects. The Army Corps of Engineers is in charge of most flood-control projects.

From the 1940s to the 1970s, "channel improvement" projects were constructed on nearly 40,000 miles (65,000 kilometers) of waterways by the Army Corps of Engineers and the SOIL CONSERVATION service. Another 190,000 miles (305,000 kilometers) were modified by local governments. The corps made extensive alterations to the Mississippi River, building levees, or walls of dirt, to divert the river. The aim was to straighten the river, making it easier for boats to navigate, and to prevent flooding.

Straightening rivers and building flood-control DAMS has had many effects that were not understood in the past. These alterations may actually increase flood hazards by permitting residents in FLOODPLAIN areas to live closer to the river than is safe. Therefore, when a dam fails, the flood causes more damage to people and homes than it would have if residents were not present. Levees are not really a means of flood control. They prevent floods in a local area, but flooding is then likely to occur either upstream or downstream. Breaks in levees can cause serious floods like those in the

◆ An employee of the Army Corps of Engineers walks along a sandbag levee known as the Burlap Wall, built to protect the historic town of St. Genevieve, Missouri, from the floods of 1993.

midwestern part of the United States in 1993.

The Army Corps of Engineers has changed the focus of its responsibility. In order to improve the ENVIRONMENT, it now spends much of its time on projects such as diverting water into WILDLIFE refuges and returning rivers to their natural state by removing flood-control dams and levees. [*See also* ROOSEVELT, FRANKLIN DELANO.]

Artesian Well

▶A hole from which water is obtained that is drilled into a deep underground rock layer where water pressure is high. The water, contained in a porous rock layer called an AQUIFER, is under pressure because it is trapped by a thick, dense layer of rock on top. It flows freely out of the well without having to be pumped. Because it comes from great depths, artesian well water is considered very pure.

Artesian wells may occur naturally at faults in Earth's crust where thick rock layers are broken. Such artesian water comes from deep volcanic rock layers and may flow out boiling hot, containing such a high MINERAL content that it cannot be used for IRRIGATION or drinking. There are major artesian rock formations in California, France, London, and Australia. [*See also* PLATE TECTONICS; WATER, DRINKING; WATER CYCLE; and WATER TABLE.]

◆ Asbestos is made of very fine particles, which can cause cancer when lodged in the lungs.

Asbestos

▶A fibrous white or light gray MINERAL that can be made into articles that are flexible, strong, and resistant to the effects of heat and acids. The material is no longer

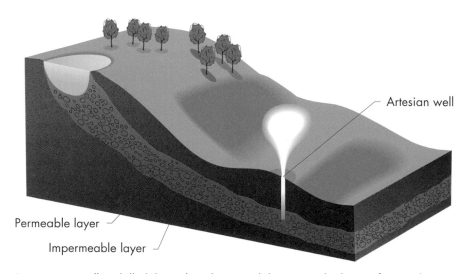

Artesian well

Permeable layer

Impermeable layer

◆ An artesian well is drilled through a dense rock layer into the layer of groundwater.

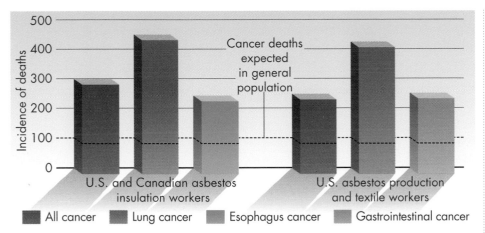

Cancer deaths expected in general population

◆ The rates of some cancers are two to four times higher for asbestos workers than they are for the general population.

used because it poses a threat to human health

Because of its resistance to heat, asbestos was widely used in the past in the manufacture of pipe insulation, brake pads, and linings for cars, hair driers, and similar items. Asbestos was once also a common additive in cement, patching plaster, and in soundproof and fireproof coatings on walls and ceilings. In recent years, people have stopped using asbestos for most of these purposes.

If the fine asbestos particles are inhaled, they can permanently lodge in the lungs. Exposure to inhaled asbestos can cause such diseases as asbestosis, or pulmonary fibrosis; mesothelioma, a CANCER of the lung lining; or lung cancer. People who work directly with asbestos are at the highest risk of disease. Because of its ill effects, the use of asbestos in insulation, fireproofing, and decoration was banned in the United States in 1974. Bans on most other uses of asbestos went into effect by 1997. [*See also* CARCINOGEN.]

Atmosphere

▶ The envelope of gases that surrounds a planet, moon, or star. Earth's atmosphere is composed mostly of the gases NITROGEN, OXYGEN, and CARBON DIOXIDE. It also contains small amounts of other gases, water vapor, and dust particles. Our planet's atmosphere sustains life by providing air to breathe and shielding life from certain kinds of hazardous RADIATION from the sun. The atmosphere also absorbs heat so that Earth never gets too hot or too cold.

Gravity keeps the atmosphere in place around the globe. The constant pull of gravity on the atmospheric components produces a relatively dense atmosphere at Earth's surface that is rich in oxygen, nitrogen, and water vapor. The atmosphere becomes less dense at high altitudes. At sea level air (barometric) pressure is 14.7 pounds per square inch, or 10.1

◆ The aurora borealis is seen in the night sky near the North Pole. The colorful waves of light result from the interaction of the ionosphere with lower atmospheric layers.

◆ The aurora borealis is also known as *northern lights* because it occurs in the northern hemisphere.

◆ Two types of cloud formations in the troposphere are cumulus and cirrocumulus clouds.

newton per square centimeter. At sea level 14.7 pounds (6.7 kilograms) of air is pressing down on every square inch (6.4 square centimeters) of your body. We do not feel this pressure because we have the same amount of air pressure inside our bodies, pressing out. However, astronauts must travel into space in pressurized capsules and wear pressurized spacesuits when they walk in the thin, low pressure of space.

Our atmosphere has four main layers—the TROPOSPHERE, the STRATOSPHERE, the MESOSPHERE, and the ionosphere.

THE TROPOSPHERE

The troposphere is the layer of the atmosphere closest to Earth. It is about 8 miles (13 kilometers) thick in the Northern and Southern hemispheres, a little thicker at the Equator—about 12 miles (19 kilometers)—and much thinner—about 4 miles (6.4 kilometers)—at the poles. Nitrogen makes up nearly four-fifths of the troposphere, with nearly one-fifth being oxygen that thins out in the upper troposphere.

The troposphere also contains a small quantity of carbon dioxide, which is essential for PLANTS. On Earth, human activity such as the burning of FOSSIL FUELS, increases the carbon dioxide content in the atmosphere. Some scientists fear that too much carbon dioxide in the atmosphere may trap the sun's heat on Earth, causing the CLIMATE to become warmer.

Earth's WEATHER is produced in the troposphere. Many specks of dust from SOIL, fires, and plants are in this layer. Water vapor collects on the dust particles, forming CLOUDS. The sun heats Earth. The heat then bounces back into the atmosphere, creating wind that moves the clouds. As the clouds rise or fall, they pick up cold air at high altitudes or warm air near Earth's surface. Strong winds in the top part of the troposphere, called jet streams, steer the weather around the globe.

Volcanic eruptions are the greatest source of dust in the troposphere. Severe cold weather and heavy snow usually occur about a year after a huge volcanic eruption.

THE STRATOSPHERE

The stratosphere is Earth's second closest atmospheric layer. It is about 20 miles (32 kilometers) thick. Near the troposphere, the stratosphere is very cold and windy, but about midway up, it becomes very warm. This warmth is due to a layer of OZONE, a gas made up of oxygen that is formed by the sun's radiation. The OZONE LAYER protects life on Earth from the sun's dangerous ULTRAVIOLET RADIATION. Scientists have found that chlorofluorocarbons (CFCS), used as propellants in many AEROSOL cans, in air conditioning, and many industries, can destroy ozone. Some fear that the continuing use of CFCs will damage the protective ozone layer.

THE MESOSPHERE AND IONOSPHERE

The mesosphere is a very cold layer that is about 20 miles (32 kilometers) thick. The mesosphere is the coldest layer of the atmosphere.

The highest layer, the ionosphere, is nearest to the sun. Here the air is very thin. The sun's radiation changes molecules of gas in this layer into electrically charged particles. Electric currents flow from particle to particle, preventing radio waves from Earth from penetrating the layer. Instead, the radio waves bounce. Thus, radio waves from one point on Earth can be bounced off the ionosphere to reach another point on Earth. However, the ionosphere can be affected by *solar flares*, which are sudden spurts of energy from the sun. When this happens, radio signals expected to arrive at one place on Earth may end up somewhere else. Colorful waves of light seen in the night sky near the Earth's two poles are the result of the interaction of the ionosphere with lower atmospheric layers. Near the North Pole, the phenomenon is known as the *aurora borealis*, or northern lights. Near the South Pole, the phenomenon is called the *aurora australis*, or southern lights. [*See also* FUEL; GLOBAL WARMING; GREENHOUSE GAS; OZONE HOLE; and VOLCANISM.]

Atmospheric Pollution

See ATMOSHERE

Atomic Energy Commission (AEC)

▶A former civilian agency (1946–1974) of the U.S. government that supervised the production and use of nuclear energy for both civilian and military applications. Congress established the AEC in 1946 and later abolished it through the Energy Reorganization Act of 1974. AEC's research operations were transferred to a new agency, the Energy Research and Development Administration (ERDA). ERDA became defunct in 1977, when its duties were assigned to the Department of Energy. The Energy Reorganization Act also created the Nuclear Regulatory Commission (NRC), an independent agency that assumed the AEC's responsibilities for licensing and monitoring construction and operation of NUCLEAR POWER plants.

Audubon, John James (1785–1851)

▶A naturalist and artist who made watercolor paintings of BIRDS, animals, flowers, and trees. Audubon's ability to capture the texture and color of his bird specimens helped convince people of the need to conserve these animals when they became threatened with EXTINCTION.

Audubon was born April 26, 1785, in what is now called Haiti. He was raised in France but moved to the United States when he was 19. He spent much of his time roaming the wooded hills HUNTING and painting near his home in Pennsylvania. His great plan was to paint all the birds of North America.

Audubon made at least 1,000 pictures of birds, most of which contain more than two individuals, 78 watercolors of MAMMALS, 100 portraits; landscape sketches; and watercolors of eggs.

Audubon predicted the destruction of WILDLIFE in America. He passionately believed that in years to come no one would ever again have the opportunity to study the birds of America and their HABITATS as he did. His works have been often reprinted, and the Audubon Society, named in his honor, was established to promote the preservation and study of wildlife. [*See also* CONSERVATION.]

Automobile

▮**A**ny kind of self-powered vehicle that can be steered by a person and used on a roadway. In its most general sense, the term *automobile* includes cars, trucks, vans, and buses.

The first "motor car," as it was called, appeared in 1896 in the United States with the development of a vehicle sold by the Duryea Motor Wagon Company of Massachusetts and the development of the Stanley Steamer by Francis Edgar and Freelan O. Stanley the same year. However, it was not until the introduction of the Model A by Henry Ford in 1903 that a gasoline-powered automobile became readily available for purchase by the public. The development of the automobile is one of the most significant inventions in human history. The vehicle provided indi-

◆ The Model T Ford was developed after the Model A. It came out in 1908 and cost $850.

◆ Exhaust from automobiles is a major air pollutant.

viduals with a means of travel that was quick, efficient, and readily available.

Since its development, the automobile has become the most widely used means of transportation in the world. This extensive use has created innumerable jobs for people working in the automotive industry as well as for those involved in the construction of roads, bridges, tunnels, and the maintenance of these structures. While this invention has provided people with great freedom in

their travel, its extensive use has also had devastating effects on the ENVIRONMENT.

Most automobiles use gasoline as their FUEL source. Gasoline is developed from PETROLEUM, a FOSSIL FUEL. As with other fossil fuels, the burning of gasoline to obtain energy releases pollutants such as CARBON MONOXIDE, CARBON DIOXIDE, and other substances into the environment. Many of these substances are toxic to humans and other organisms. They also contribute to such unwanted environmental

◆ Because of the environmental problems associated with the use of gasoline-powered automobiles, many experiments use alternative fuel sources.

Autotroph

▌An organism that can synthesize complex food molecules from simple inorganic materials in their ENVIRONMENT. Autotrophs, also known as PRODUCERS, form the basis of all FOOD CHAINS. All animals and other organisms, such as FUNGI, that cannot make their own food ultimately depend on autotrophs as their food source.

PLANTS are the most familiar autotrophs, manufacturing food through the chemical reactions of PHOTOSYNTHESIS. Other photosynthetic autotrophs include ALGAE and the chlorophyll-containing BACTERIA. Chemosynthetic bacteria are autotrophs that produce food in the dark through a series of chemical reactions. Such bacteria play a role in the NITROGEN CYCLE. Chemosynthetic bacteria are also producers for certain deep-sea ECOSYSTEMS centered on hot springs on the OCEAN floor. [See also CONSUMER; FOOD WEB; and HERBIVORE.]

conditions as the development of SMOG, GLOBAL WARMING, and ACID RAIN. In addition, the extensive use of petroleum products to power automobiles has drastically decreased the amounts of petroleum, a NONRENEWABLE RESOURCE, available for use in the future.

To combat some of the environmental problems associated with the use of automobiles, individuals, governments, and scientists are seeking alternate means of transportation for people as well as ALTERNATIVE ENERGY SOURCES to power automobiles. In many communities, the use of MASS TRANSIT is encouraged as a way to reduce the number of automobiles on the road, and thus reduce the amounts of pollutants released into the environment. Moreover, the federal government has required that devices such as CATALYTIC CONVERTERS be installed on automobiles to reduce the amounts of pollutants they release. To help conserve dwindling petroleum supplies, some scientists have experimented with the use of fuels such as GASOHOL to power automobiles. This fuel has the advantage of using some RENEWABLE RESOURCES in its production. In addition, scientists have experimented with and produced automobiles that are powered by SOLAR ENERGY. Thus far, these automobiles have not been mass-produced because they cannot travel as far or as fast as conventional automobiles. Increasing government restrictions on fuel efficiency and the amounts of pollutants that individual automobiles can release into the environment are likely to result in future automobiles that are very different from those of today. [See also CLEAN AIR ACT; GREENHOUSE EFFECT; GREENHOUSE GAS; and POLLUTION.]

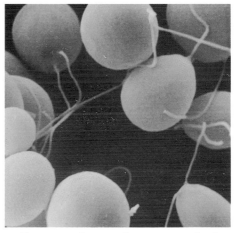

◆ Algae are photosynthetic autotrophs that supply animals with food and oxygen.

B

Bacteria

DVariety of one-celled organisms that have no **nucleus**. Bacteria are often called microbes; however, not all microbes are also bacteria. Microbes are a variety of one-celled organisms, including protists and simple FUNGI, as well as VIRUSES. Protists and fungi have an envelope, or nucleus, inside their cells, which contains most of their deoxyribonucleic acid, or DNA. Bacteria differ from these organisms because they do not have a nucleus enclosing their DNA.

Bacteria and other microbes make up a large part of the living matter on Earth. On 1 acre (0.4 hectare) of fertile SOIL, there may be as much as 500 pounds (227 kilograms) of microbes. Many of these are bacteria that perform a great variety of jobs in the ENVIRONMENT. In fact, bacteria are very important parts of ECOSYSTEMS

everywhere. Some bacteria cause illness in or kill PLANTS, animals, or people. However, such harmful bacteria are greatly outnumbered by bacteria that recycle nutrients, break down wastes, or produce useful materials.

CLASSIFICATION OF BACTERIA

Thousands of SPECIES of bacteria are grouped according to their shapes. The *cocci* are generally round; the *bacilli* are generally rod shaped; and the *spirilla* have a spiral or corkscrew shape. Within these groups, some bacteria are brightly colored; some have structures that look like tails or propellers; some glow in the dark; and a few species are even square.

Cyanobacteria are a group whose cells contain the green pigment called *chlorophyll*. Chlorophyll is used to carry out PHOTOSYNTHESIS. Cyanobacteria are often called blue-green ALGAE.

Like other living things, bacteria pass their traits to their offspring in their GENES. Over many generations, changes may occur in the genes that are passed on, allowing the bacteria to evolve and develop into new species. Compared to larger organisms, bacteria can evolve rather quickly, especially if the environment is changing. This is partly because populations of bacteria often number in the millions or billions and go through dozens of generations in a day. With so many new individuals appearing so quickly, there is a fairly good chance that mutants will turn up. A **mutant** might have genes that are better for living in the changed environment. This individual will grow and multiply rapidly. Soon bacteria with these same genes will become common in the population. Thus, a population of bacteria often adjusts to new foods, toxins, or other conditions in a short time. As a result, bacteria are much less likely to become extinct than are larger species, such as ELEPHANTS, that cannot adjust so quickly to changes.

BACTERIA ECOSYSTEM

Bacteria are one of the most adaptable forms of life. They grow almost anywhere there is water—in damp soil, in and on plants and animals, inside machines, and in rocks thousands of feet below ground. Bacteria also live in ponds, lakes, OCEANS, and even in CLOUDS.

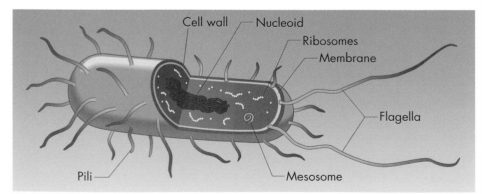

Cell wall — Nucleoid

Ribosomes

Membrane

Flagella

Pili

Mesosome

◆ A typical rod-shaped bacterium. Bacteria are so small that several trillion could fit in a container the size of the screw-on cap of a soda bottle.

THE LANGUAGE OF THE ENVIRONMENT

mutant an organism that is different from its parents because of a change, called a *mutation*, in the genes that are inherited from them; a mutant may be better suited or less suited than its parents to life in a particular environment.

nucleus the center of a cell.

spores an inactive form of bacterium that survives for a long period without food.

Even where bacteria cannot grow, they are often present as inactive **spores**. Bacteria are able to live at the highest and lowest temperatures tolerated by any living thing. Almost anything, from human skin to concrete, is food for some species of bacteria. In addition, many poisons, from PESTICIDES to RADIOACTIVE WASTE, are tolerated by some species of bacteria.

Nutrient Cycling

Without bacteria, nutrients such as nitrogen, sulfur, and CARBON would be harder for plants and animals to obtain. Many of these nutrients might be nearby, but they might not be in a form that a plant can absorb or an animal can eat. Fortunately, the action of bacteria and other microbes helps make nutrients available and helps circulate them in an ecosystem.

Some bacteria are DECOMPOSERS, which break down dead organisms and waste and release nutrients that living organisms reuse. Others capture nutrients from the air or from rock and change them into forms that living things can use. For example, bacteria and cyanobacteria in the soil capture nitrogen from the ATMOSPHERE in large amounts. The nitrogen is changed by the bacteria into ammonia and nitrates that are used by plants. Without this process of NITROGEN FIXING, many ecosystems would be far less productive than they are. Also, much of the CARBON DIOXIDE in the atmosphere is produced

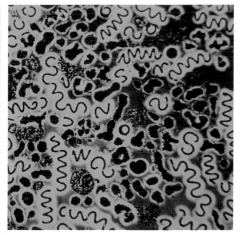
Cyanobacteria

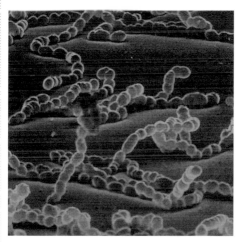
Streptococcus

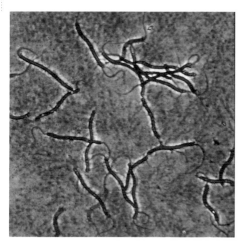
Spirillum volutans

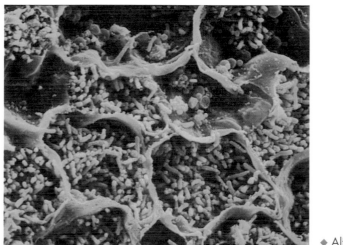

◆ Alfalfa nodules have nitrogen-fixing bacteria.

◆ Bacteria come in a variety of shapes and exist in almost every type of habitat.

Bacteria 49

by bacterial decomposers. The carbon dioxide helps plants grow and affects the temperature of the planet.

Bacteria Inside Organisms

Many organisms depend directly on bacteria for their survival. Plants such as clover and beans are nourished by nitrogen-fixing bacteria that live in their roots. Some deep-sea FISH have bacteria that glow in the dark while growing in their skin. These bacteria help the fish see and communicate with one another. Animals, including people, have billions of bacteria living in their digestive systems. Many of these bacteria help break down food, make vitamins available, and perform other biological processes.

In contrast, some bacteria cause deadly diseases in WILDLIFE or people. Disease outbreaks, or epidemics, sometimes reduce populations of animals, especially if a population is unusually large or crowded. The Black Plague was a bacterial disease that killed about a third of the people in Europe during one epidemic in the fourteenth century. Today, other bacterial diseases, such as tuberculosis and cholera, are still concerns for humans, especially for people living in crowded or dirty conditions.

BACTERIA AS HUMAN TOOLS

Bacteria are NATURAL RESOURCES that have been used by people even before they knew bacteria existed. For centuries, milk products such as yogurt and some cheeses have been made using bacteria. Soil bacteria have always been important in agriculture.

During the last two centuries, much has been learned about bacteria, and we are beginning to use them in many new ways. For example, they are used to make medicines, to produce chemicals for medicical and industrial purposes, and as water purification agents in SEWAGE TREATMENT PLANTS. Some of the most exciting new uses of bacteria are in the fields of BIOREMEDIATION, biotechnology, and GENETIC ENGINEERING.

In these new technologies, bacteria are used for cleaning up TOXIC WASTE or for moving genes from one living thing to another to create organisms that perform special tasks. There is some concern that the practice of changing the genes of organisms is dangerous because harmful bacteria could be made by accident. However, bacteria acquire new genes quite often under natural conditions. Humans might only be adding to a process that happens already. In any case, both the natural activities of bacteria and the uses of bacteria by people will continue to have a huge impact on people and the environment. [*See also* BIOGEOCHEMICAL CYCLE; CARBON CYCLE; COMPOSTING; HEALTH AND DISEASE; LEGUME; NITROGEN CYCLE; and PATHOGEN.]

Bald Eagle

Predatory BIRD of North America, recognized as the national symbol of the United States. The bald

eagle, a member of the bird family *Accipitridae,* is one of North America's largest birds, with a body length of about 40 inches (1 meter) and a wingspan of up to 7.5 feet (2.3 meters). Adult bald eagles are dark brown and black with a white head and neck and a white tail.

Bald eagles live near freshwater HABITATS. They build their large nests on cliffs and at the tops of tall trees near these waterways. As predatory birds, bald eagles feed primarily on FISH, rodents, and other small animals.

Bald eagles used to be found over most of North America, particularly in the United States. Today, populations of bald eagles have been drastically reduced and are found mostly in parts of Canada and the northern United States. They are now listed as an ENDANGERED SPECIES in all states except Michigan, Minnesota, Oregon, Washington, and Wisconsin, where they are listed as a threatened SPECIES. Alaska is the only state where the bald eagle is not listed as endangered or threatened.

HUNTING OF BALD EAGLES

Scientists have identified several reasons for the decrease in the number of bald eagles in North America. HUNTING had the earliest impact. Before colonization of North America by the European settlers, many Native American groups killed bald eagles because they believed that eagles held spiritual powers. The feathers, wings, and claws of bald eagles were collected and used for ceremonial purposes.

Colonization of North America introduced many more problems for bald eagles. As settlers cut down FORESTS for towns and farmlands, bald eagles lost their nesting places. They were also seen as a danger to lambs, calves, and other LIVESTOCK. To rid the area of eagles, hunters shot, trapped, and poisoned the birds. Some even raided the nests for eggs.

Many bald eagles were also killed indirectly by LEAD poisoning. Lead poisoning continues to be a problem for bald eagles today. Many hunters use lead shot to hunt waterfowl, such as ducks and geese. Sometimes, the lead pellets left in the ENVIRONMENT are eaten as grit. The grit is used for grinding food in their gizzards. Poisoned by the lead, the birds become disabled and are easy prey for bald eagles. After eating the contaminated birds, the eagles become poisoned, too.

EFFECTS OF DDT

Perhaps the biggest reason for the drop in the bald eagle population occurred in the twentieth century.

After World War II, farmers began to use the chemical dichloro-diphenyl trichloroethane (DDT) to protect crops and trees from damage by INSECTS. DDT is a very effective PESTICIDE that was used widely in the agricultural industry.

For more than 20 years, DDT was used without regard to the possible damage it could cause to the environment. When environmental scientists began to study DDT, they determined that it has several side effects. Among these is the fact that DDT does not

break down in the environment quickly. When animals or other organisms eat or absorb DDT, it is stored by the body. The stored DDT can be passed along the FOOD CHAIN, in increasingly higher concentrations, as animals eat each other. This process is known as BIOACCUMULATION.

Bioaccumulation has its greatest effect on the top CARNIVORE of a food chain, such as the bald eagle. In birds, DDT interferes with the reproductive process by causing females to lay eggs with very thin

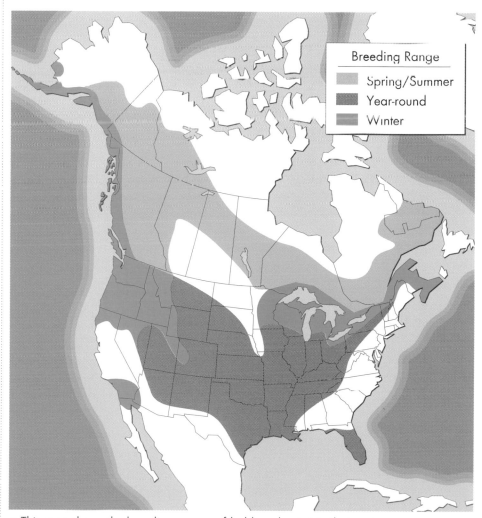

◆ This map shows the breeding ranges of bald eagles in North America.

shells. These shells are easily broken, killing the developing embryos.

PROTECTING BALD EAGLES

In 1972, the United States recognized DDT as a harmful chemical and banned its use throughout the country. This ban was a turning point in the recovery of the bald eagle population. In 1973, bald eagles were one of the first species protected under the ENDANGERED SPECIES ACT. Since that time, the bald eagle has been helped by recovery programs and programs that protect its habitat. Bald eagle populations are slowly recovering in some states. In 1994, the U.S. FISH AND WILDLIFE SERVICE moved the bald eagle from the endangered to the threatened species list in several states. [*See also* EXTINCTION and WATER POLLUTION.]

Barrier Islands

DLands surrounded by water that are separated from the mainland coast by a channel. Because of their locations, barrier islands help protect the mainland coast from damage caused by the full force of OCEAN waves and storms.

Though usually composed of loose SEDIMENT, such as sand and gravel, barrier islands exist in an offshore ENVIRONMENT of shifting tides, waves, and winds. The islands may change shape because of

◆ Barrier islands in North Carolina help protect the state's coasts.

storms or gradually move if there is a change in sea level. Despite such changes, barrier islands persist. They can do so because of a balance that exists between the EROSION and the **deposition** of island material by wind and waves.

People and WILDLIFE benefit from the shelter provided to coastal areas by barrier islands. The value this environment provides to both groups often creates conflicts in island management. For example, barrier beaches and **dunes** provide recreation areas for people and nesting HABITAT for coastal BIRDS. Calm, shallow water on the landward side of these islands provides conditions in which SALT MARSHES may develop. At the same time, the conditions are also ideal for

the building of marinas that may destroy habitat for marsh organisms.

Largely because of their beauty and nearness to the ocean, barrier islands attract large numbers of people. This creates a demand for permanent buildings and roads on these islands. However, such construction conflicts with the normal, unrestrained movement of the sand. In addition, such structures are frequently destroyed by hurricanes and tropical storms. [*See also* ESTUARY; NATIONAL SEASHORE; and NATURAL DISASTERS.]

Best Available Control Technology (BACT)

▶ Emission standards required by the ENVIRONMENTAL PROTECTION AGENCY (EPA) for all new or modified sources of AIR POLLUTION in areas meeting the National Ambient Air Quality Standard (NAAQS). Best Available Control Technology (BACT) can include the overall design and layout of a factory or power plant, its pollution control equipment, and its operational procedures. Under laws in the CLEAN AIR ACT, any **stationary source** of POLLUTION, such as a factory or power plant, must apply for a permit to release air pollutants. To create new sources of air pollution, applicants must show that **emission** levels will not violate NAAQS or the Clean Air Act of 1970. According to the permit, applicants must use BACT for each type of pollutant released.

BACT standards apply to all new structures as well as to existing ones. Under the Clean Air Act, if a new stationary source cannot meet BACT standards because of financial or other reasons, then it must meet the New Source Performance Standards (NSPS). Determined by the EPA, the NSPS takes into consideration the cost of pollution control. BACT standards, on the other hand, are determined without regard to cost.

BACT standards have resulted in significant reductions in air pollution. Since the standards were

◆ This coal-fired power plant is equipped with air pollution control units used to control emission levels.

THE LANGUAGE OF THE ENVIRONMENT

emission a substance that is discharged into the environment

stationary source a permanent fixed structure, such as a power plant or factory, that gives off pollutants.

put into effect after the passage of the Clean Air Act in 1970, the EPA reports that pollution has decreased by more than 25%, and pollution from PARTICULATES has dropped by more than 50%. [*See also* ACID RAIN; AIR POLLUTION CONTROL ACT (1955); NITROGEN DIOXIDE; POLLUTION PERMITS; and PRIMARY POLLUTION.]

Best Practical Technology

See BEST AVAILABLE CONTROL TECHNOLOGY (BACT)

Bhopal Incident

▶ An accident in Bhopal, India, in 1984 at a Union Carbide plant in which toxic gas was released, injuring and killing thousands of people. On December 3, 1984, a storage tank at a pesticide plant in Bhopal, India, began to leak. It contained a deadly chemical called *methylisocyanate* (MIC). MIC is used to make the pesticide Sevin. As the MIC escaped from the tank, it changed into a gas. Plant workers were unable to stop the leak or neutralize the gas. By the time the tank emptied its contents, the poisonous gas had spread over 25 square miles (65 square kilometers).

The gas that leaked from the tank killed 8,000 residents of Bhopal. An additional 300,000 people suffered damage to their eyes, brains, immune systems, kidneys, intestines, or livers. Many of the people injured died within a few years. Women who were pregnant at the time of the leak gave birth to dead or deformed babies.

Before the Bhopal incident occurred, a journalist wrote several articles about the lack of safety procedures in the plant. The articles included a report about an accident in which five workers were injured by an MIC leak in 1982. The articles were ignored. The journalist also went to legislators and the Indian Supreme Court with his concerns. Again his information was ignored. Finally, the journalist wrote an article for *Jansatta,* the Indian national newspaper, in which he predicted that an MIC leak would kill everyone in Bhopal. The article was published shortly before the disaster.

It was not until many people were killed or injured by a leak from the plant that people began

◆ Thousands of animals perished as a result of the accidental release of poisonous gas from the Union Carbide plant in Bhopal, India.

to question the safety practices of such plants. An investigation showed that the factory lacked an automatic safety system. The management of the plant believed a manual safety system was better because it created more jobs. Twice, Union Carbide officials from Danbury, Connecticut, had advised the plant manager and the town officials to develop a system to alert and evacuate people from the plant area if an emergency situation occurred. However, nothing was done. In addition, the Bhopal board did not have the instruments needed to measure emissions from the plant. When the board received reports that cows had died because

of discharge from the plant's drainage system, months before the leak, it took no action.

The chemical leak in Bhopal was one of the worst industrial accidents in history. The disaster raised questions worldwide about where such factories should be located, the safety procedures they use, and how they affect the employees of the companies. Following the incident, the plant was closed. In addition, many countries began to pressure the United Nations to set up regulations that would ensure the safe use of chemical technology brought to developing nations by developed nations. [*See also* AGRICULTURAL POLLUTION.]

Bioaccumulation

D The gradual increase in the concentration of certain chemicals in the tissues of organisms. Bioaccumulation, also called biomagnification, is most often a problem in aquatic ECOSYSTEMS. Such ecosystems have vast FOOD WEBS that can include hundreds of SPECIES. Bioaccumulation begins when a PESTICIDE such as dichlorodiphenyl trichloroethane (DDT) is washed from farmland into a nearby body of water. Even in small amounts, the chemical can be absorbed by ALGAE or eaten by tiny animals and other microorganisms. These chemicals are passed along the FOOD CHAIN each time an organism eats another. Over time, as an organism continues eating contaminated SPECIES, the chemicals accumulate in the feeding organism's tissues and increase in concentration. Eventually, the chemicals may harm the organism or its offspring.

The concentration of chemical substances in the tissues of organisms increases at each higher level of the food chain. Thus, the bioaccumulation of pesticides has the greatest effect on the top CARNIVORE of a food chain. In the case of DDT, high concentrations can kill an animal; severely damage its immune system, the body system that helps an organism fight diseases; or impair its ability to reproduce.

One of the most serious consequences of bioaccumulation has resulted from the use of DDT. Bioaccumulation of this pesticide in several species of predatory birds caused the shells of the eggs laid by these birds to become thin and brittle. When eggshells become too thin, they break before the embryos inside fully develop. As a result, the embryos die and the population of the species decreases. This problem is one reason why populations of BALD EAGLES and peregrine falcons became so low that these bird species were in danger of EXTINCTION.

After several years of study and debate, in 1972 scientists convinced the U.S. government that bioaccumulation was a major side effect resulting from the use of DDT. Using the endangered bald eagle as an example, the scientists convinced the U.S. government to ban its use as a pesticide. Today, bald eagles and other species have benefited from the 1972 ban on DDT. Populations of these animals are slowly recovering. In 1994, bald eagles were moved from the ENDANGERED SPECIES list to the less-critical threatened species list. [*See also* ENDANGERED SPECIES ACT and WATER POLLUTION.]

Biochemical Oxygen Demand (BOD)

D A measure of the amount of organic material, such as SEWAGE, in water. The calculation is determined by measuring the amount of OXYGEN consumed when a BIO

◆ The bioaccumulation of DDT in organisms can cause the shell of the egg laid by the bald eagle to be thin, preventing the embryo from developing.

DEGRADABLE substance is oxidized, or combined with oxygen, in water. The higher the biochemical oxygen demand of polluted water, the more organic matter it contains. Raw sewage has a BOD of 40–150 milligrams per liter. Water clean enough for humans to drink has a BOD of less than 0.5 milligrams per liter. [*See also* WATER, DRINKING; WATER QUALITY STANDARDS; and WATER TREATMENT.]

Biodegradable

Able to be broken down by living organisms into simpler chemicals. The process by which biodegradable materials are broken down is known as DECOMPOSITION. Decomposition occurs when BACTERIA, FUNGI, or other organisms digest substances.

Most biodegradable products are made from natural, carbon-based, organic materials. Examples of such materials include living things and products made from them. When living things die, they are decomposed by microorganisms. In this process, large compounds are broken down to form nutrients that can be used again by PLANTS and other organisms. Decomposition prevents Earth from becoming cluttered with the remains of organisms.

Many products humans use and throw away are biodegradable. Such products include cardboard, newspaper, paper bags, cotton fibers, leather and other natural fabrics, and food wastes.

BENEFITS OF BIODEGRADABLE PRODUCTS

The main benefit of using biodegradable products is that such products are relatively safe for the ENVIRONMENT. The LEACHING of toxic chemicals from GARBAGE is one problem associated with LANDFILLS. When water seeps down through a landfill, it can mix with chemicals from PESTICIDES, batteries, cleansers, appliances, and other products. This mixture, called *leachate,* can sometimes enter groundwater supplies, making water unsafe for drinking, cooking, or bathing. In contrast, biodegradable products are made mostly of organic materials. They can be broken down by DECOMPOSERS, recycling the material back into a FOOD CHAIN. This reduces the amount of material that must be stored long term in landfills, and naturally recycles resources.

Available landfill space in the United States is being used up rapidly. According to the U.S. ENVIRONMENTAL PROTECTION AGENCY (EPA), 25 states might be without sufficient landfill space for garbage disposal by the year 2000. If environmental conditions are good for decomposition, though, many biodegradable products decompose in a short amount of time. These rapidly decomposing wastes add to the garbage problem for only a short period of time.

Products made from non-biodegradable substances may remain in the environment for hundreds of years. Synthetic materials, such as PLASTICS, polyester, and nylon, cannot be broken down by microorganisms. Instead, these materials accumulate layer upon layer in landfills and other areas.

◆ Natural materials, such as grass cuttings, are biodegradable.

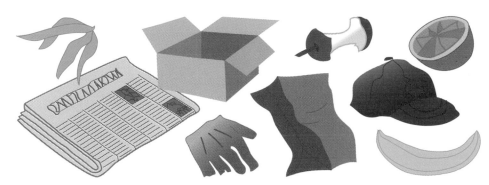

◆ Many things used by people are biodegradable.

◆ Because they are organic, the leaves and stems of peppermint, used to make peppermint oil, are not harmful to the environment when dumped.

DEGRADABLE PLASTICS

Through advances in science and technology, many companies are now selling products made from degradable plastics. One type of degradable plastic is made by blending cornstarch into the plastic. This plastic partially decomposes when microorganisms feed upon the cornstarch in the material. Over time, the plastic weakens and falls apart into many small pieces. Although adding cornstarch to plastic aids in breaking the plastic apart, critics of these plastics emphasize that the smaller pieces of plastic remain in the environment for many years. The plastic does not disappear; it is merely spread around.

An alternative to plastics that is becoming popular is a foamlike material made of cornstarch. This material is commonly used to make the packing "peanuts" used to fill boxes to be shipped. These foamlike peanuts are nontoxic. They also dissolve quickly when they come in contact with water. [*See also* COMPOSTING; DECOMPOSER; PETROLEUM; PHOTODEGRADABLE PLASTIC; RECYCLING, REDUCING, REUSING; SEWAGE TREATMENT PLANT; SOURCE REDUCTION; and WASTE MANAGEMENT.]

Biodiversity

The variety of PLANTS, animals, and other living things on Earth. Although biological diversity, or biodiversity, is usually thought of in terms of numbers of different SPECIES, it also applies to the variation within a single species, as well as to an entire ECOSYSTEM.

VARIETY IN NATURE

Biodiversity usually refers to SPECIES DIVERSITY, the number of different species that exist in the world. According to the biologist Edward Osborne WILSON, scientists have identified more than 1 million different species of living things. This number includes all plants, animals, FUNGI, and other **organisms,** such as BACTERIA and ALGAE. By far the most abundant and diverse types of living things are INSECTS. In fact, the insect world is filled with such variety that there may actually be more types of beetles than plants!

Amazingly, most scientists agree that the 1.4 million species known to humans is only an estimate. It is possible that between 10 and 100 million other species await discovery in the unexplored regions of the world. According to

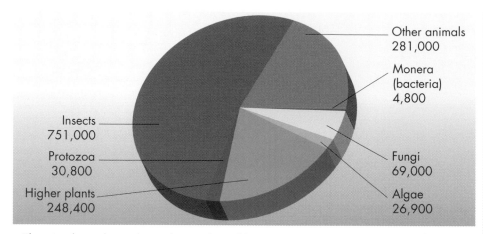

Insects
751,000

Protozoa
30,800

Higher plants
248,400

Other animals
281,000

Monera
(bacteria)
4,800

Fungi
69,000

Algae
26,900

◆ The pie chart above shows the number of known species, in major groups of organisms. Insect species are by far the most numerous.

Wilson, the great majority of these will be found in tropical RAIN FORESTS, where the number of species is rivaled only by the number found in CORAL REEFS. For instance, a study has shown that nearly twice as many species of BIRDS live in the tiny, tropical country of Panama as in the entire United States.

DIFFERENCE AMONG GENES

Another type of biodiversity is GENETIC DIVERSITY—the variety of differences that exists within a single species. Familiar examples of genetic diversity are the numerous breeds of dogs and cats and the different shapes and sizes of students in an eighth-grade science class.

Minor differences between individuals within a species result from differences in their GENES. All living things have genes, the portions of a cell's chromosomes that carry information for specific traits, such as hair or fur color, leaf shape, and body size.

If a species has a good deal of genetic diversity, it is more likely to survive a changing or altered ENVIRONMENT. Some members of a population may be better suited to the environment than others. These individuals will pass their helpful genes to their offspring and thereby carry on the species. A species with low genetic diversity, on the other hand, is less likely to adapt successfully to changes in the environment and is more likely to become extinct.

Today, farmers take advantage of the fact that many food crop species, such as wheat and corn, have great genetic diversity. Wild varieties of wheat, for instance, are much more resistant to CLIMATE CHANGES, disease, and insects than are domestic varieties. Farmers can produce more desirable traits in their crops by crossbreeding domestic and wild plants. For example, in 1978, a variety of wild corn was discovered in Mexico. By crossbreeding this corn with local varieties, farmers were able to avoid costly season-to-season plowing and sowing. Crossbreeding also offered

resistance to several VIRUSES that attacked the local corn.

MANY KINDS OF ECOSYSTEMS

The third meaning of biodiversity is ecosystem diversity. This refers to the variety of ecosystems that exist on our planet, such as DESERTS, evergreen FORESTS, and SALT MARSHES. Ecosystems serve many functions. For example, they affect CLIMATE, break down wastes, and help regulate the WATER CYCLE and CARBON CYCLE. Ecosystems help keep SOILS fertile and can prevent EROSION. In addition, they provide people with food, other useful products, and scenic beauty.

Different ecosystems play different roles in the BIOSPHERE.

◆ The mouse opossum feeds at pools of water held by bromeliads, plants that live on trees in the tropical rain forest, where the greatest variety of species lives.

Coastal WETLANDS, for instance, help remove pollutants from water. They also provide feeding grounds and nurseries for a great variety of FISH and other aquatic species. The deep and extensive web of roots under forest ecosystems, on the other hand, helps prevent floods and soil erosion and keeps more water available for plants during dry seasons.

EXTINCTION: VANISHING SPECIES

Scientists are far from unlocking all the many secrets of Earth's great variety of living things. Meanwhile, the biodiversity of species, genes, and ecosystems on our planet is shrinking rapidly. Studies carried out since the 1960s show that EXTINCTION of a great many species is taking place. According to some estimates, plant and animal species are currently disappearing faster than at any other time in the last 65 million years.

Extinction of species is a natural process that usually happens in response to environmental changes. Species of plants, animals, and microscopic organisms that cannot adapt to the new environmental conditions die off. In fact, many scientists agree that the MASS EXTINCTION of dinosaurs that occurred 65 million years ago may have happened because of environmental changes that resulted from a meteor striking Earth.

Mass extinctions due to environmental changes have already occurred five times during Earth's history, but scientists today point to a different cause for the current round of mass extinctions—humans. Humans contribute to the extinction of species by destroying habitats, through activities such as hunting, and by introducing **nonnative species** to new environments.

MAINTAINING THE DIVERSITY OF LIFE

Over the course of Earth's history, many species have appeared, flourished for a time, and then become extinct. In fact, some scientists estimate that most of the species that have ever lived are now extinct. Programs to protect species on the verge of extinction, such as CAPTIVE PROPAGATION programs, are difficult to carry out, expensive, and often unsuccessful. Why then should people work to protect the Earth's biodiversity?

Perhaps the main reason for preserving biodiversity is that a wide variety of species helps keep ecosystems healthy. Healthy ecosystems, in turn, ensure a healthy biosphere by regulating the flow of energy and the cycling of important elements, such as OXYGEN,

Medicine	Plant Source	Use
Colchicine	Autumn crocus	cancer prevention
Digitalis	Common foxglove	heart stimulant
L-dopa	Velvet bean	treatment of Parkinson's disease
Penicillin	Penicillium fungus	antibiotic
Quinine	Yellow cinchona	antimalarial agent
Resperine	Indian snakeroot	lowering of blood pressure
Taxol	Pacific yew	anticancer agent
Vinblastine	Rosy periwinkle	anticancer agent

◆ The table above lists examples of common medicines and their plant sources.

CARBON, nitrogen, and water. Each species plays a key role in its ecosystem, and each is dependent on other species for survival. The ways that species depend on and interact with other species are not always obvious. What is obvious, however, is that once a species becomes extinct, it is gone forever. Since scientists have yet to discover and understand the complexities of all ecosystems, it is impossible to predict how an ecosystem will be affected by the loss of a species.

Another concern of scientists is the loss of possible sources of medicines. Currently, about 40% of all medicines used in the United States come from plants. For example, quinine, a drug used in the treatment of malaria, comes from the yellow cinchona plant. Digitalis, a medicine used to treat heart disease, comes from the common foxglove plant. Researchers are currently studying the leaves of the periwinkle plant and the bark of the Pacific yew tree, both of which show promise in the treatment of CANCER. No one knows how many more medicines lie undiscovered among Earth's biodiversity. Pharmaceutical companies are spending millions of dollars to find out.

Organisms not yet discovered may become useful in the future as food. Wild varieties can also be crossed with domestic crops to produce new varieties that are resistant to damage by insects and disease. In fact, the valuable species of Mexican wild corn that was discovered in 1978 was so rare that it was found growing on a patch of land of only 300 acres (121 hectares). Human activity and the feeding of GRAZING animals could easily have wiped out this critical species before it was put to its important use. [*See also* CONSERVATION; ENDANGERED SPECIES; ENVIRONMENTAL EDUCATION; EVOLUTION; EXOTIC SPECIES; GREEN REVOLUTION; and NATURAL SELECTION.]

Biogeochemical Cycle

The flow of chemical elements, particularly of nutrients essential to life, from organism to physical ENVIRONMENT to organism. A familiar example of the circular pathways elements follow is the CARBON CYCLE, which stabilizes CARBON DIOXIDE and OXYGEN levels in the ATMOSPHERE. For instance, animals and PLANTS both use up oxygen and release carbon dioxide when burning food to produce energy. Green plants, however, use carbon dioxide when they trap energy from the sun in PHOTOSYNTHESIS. Both plants and animals also use carbon dioxide and oxygen when creating more living matter. When organisms die, these chemicals are consumed by other organisms or released back into the ENVIRONMENT. The result of all of these processes is the cycling of the chemicals needed to sustain life.

Our planet's crust, atmosphere, OCEANS, and SOILS are pools of nutrients that are continually being transported by winds, OCEAN CURRENTS, streams and rivers, groundwater, rain, GLACIERS, and moving organisms. The basic components of any biogeochemical cycle are a large inorganic reservoir pool and a smaller active pool. The form, quantity, and location of an element varies as a result of exchanges between the reservoir pool and the active pool and within the active pool itself. Exchange between the pools is generally slow. However, in the active pool, the nutrient element in question exchanges rapidly and directly between organisms and the physical environment. The processes that cause exchanges can be physical, such as WEATHERING, or biological, such as protein synthesis and DECOMPOSITION. All these process help maintain balance in the cycle.

MINING, land drainage, SEWAGE disposal, and other human activities can affect the rate of exchange between the reservoir pool and the active pool. An excess released into the active pool disturbs the cycle's balance and may produce chemical POLLUTION such as excess sulfur in ACID RAIN or phosphorus in EUTROPHICATION.

Another kind of imbalance in a biogeochemical cycle is caused by DEFORESTATION. Without trees and other plants, carbon dioxide, a heat-trapping gas, builds up in the atmosphere. Because plants give off oxygen and water, the climate in a deforested region becomes drier as well as hotter. Many people, scientists and nonscientists alike, are concerned that a point may be reached at which very high carbon dioxide levels worldwide will trigger a runaway GREENHOUSE EFFECT. [*See also* BIOSPHERE; ECOSYSTEM; NITROGEN CYCLE; OXYGEN CYCLE; and WATER CYCLE.]

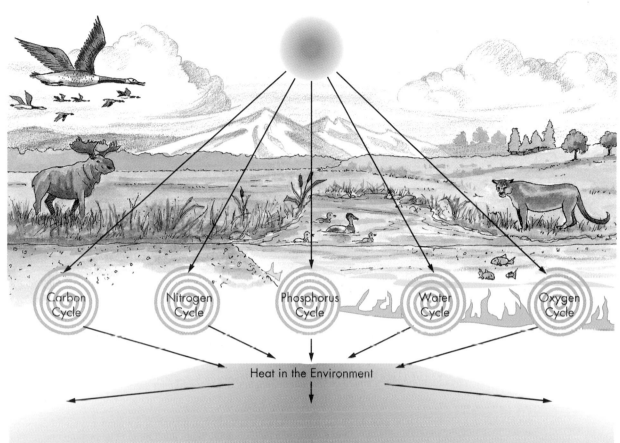

◆ Carbon, nitrogen, phosphorus, water, and oxygen cycles are all biogeochemical cycles.

Biological Community

▌All of the **populations** of organisms living together in a particular area and interacting with one another in various ways. For example, a pond community includes the populations of all the different PLANTS, FISH, INSECTS, AMPHIBIANS, BIRDS, REPTILES, MAMMALS, and **microorganisms** that live in and around the pond. The microorganisms may include BACTERIA and FUNGI, some types of ALGAE, and other protist, or protogoan, SPECIES.

STRUCTURE OF BIOLOGICAL COMMUNITIES

In large part, the kinds of species that make up a particular biological community are determined by the CLIMATE. Climate refers to WEATHER conditions—PRECIPITATION, humidity, and wind patterns—in an area. Climate has an enormous impact on the physical, or abiotic, factors of an ECOSYSTEM—amount of sunlight, availability of water, and SOIL quality—that organisms depend upon for survival.

Biological communities can be quite diverse. However, because species adapt to local environmental conditions, members of a biological community often share

characteristics. For instance, many of the animals that live in GRASSLANDS possess ADAPTATIONS, such as specialized teeth and skeletons, for feeding on grasses and moving in open territory. Similarly, most plants in DESERT communities have adaptations for conserving water, such as thick, fleshy stems that store water and waxy coverings that prevent water loss.

INTERACTIONS WITHIN BIOLOGICAL COMMUNITIES

Populations of organisms do not exist in isolation. Rather, species within a biological community depend upon resources from the

◆ The fish, plants, and other organisms that live in the ocean are all part of a biological community.

environment and often interact with each other in surprising and sometimes bizarre ways.

Predation

One of the most familiar types of interactions is predation, a relationship in which one organism kills and eats another organism. The species that is eaten is called the prey, and the one that does the eating is called the PREDATOR. Some familiar examples of predation include lions feeding on zebras, squirrels munching on acorns, and birds eating insects.

Predator-prey relationships form the basis of an ecosystem's FOOD WEB. Each time an organism eats another organism, energy is transferred from one species to the next. The predator-prey relationship is also important for the regulation of population size. Sometimes predators control the population size of their prey. More commonly, the number of prey animals or plants limits the possible

◆ In a biological community, several types of interactions occur among the organisms living in it.

◆ A biological community includes all the different types of organisms in an ecosystem.

Biological Control

▶The use of living organisms or naturally occurring chemicals to limit the number of pest organisms in an area. Biological control is an alternative to the use of **synthetic** PESTICIDES that can harm people and WILDLIFE. Many farmers used biological control methods before World War II but switched to synthetic pesticides when they became widely available.

Today, concern about the ENVIRONMENT has resulted in the development of many new biological control methods. One method is to use a pest's natural enemies against it—the PREDATORS, parasites, or PATHOGENS that normally limit the size of a pest population. Another is to make use of the chemicals that PLANTS produce naturally to defend

size of the predator's population. When prey populations decrease in size, predator populations also decrease due to lack of food.

Competition

Another important interrelationship occurs when species compete with each other for the same resources. When lions and hyenas fight over an animal carcass, they are in COMPETITION for food. Other examples of competition include dandelions and grass plants competing for water and nutrients on a patch of lawn and young trees competing for limited sunlight on a FOREST floor. Sometimes competition results in the disappearance of some populations from an ecosystem.

Partnerships Between Species

Some of the more interesting interactions within biological communities occur when species benefit in some way through close relationships with other organisms. In a relationship known as PARASITISM, one organism benefits by feeding on the cells, tissues, or fluids of

another organism (the **host**) without immediately killing it. (If the feeding organism were to kill its host organism, the feeding organism would lose its food supply.) The ticks and fleas sometimes found on dogs and cats are familiar examples of parasites, the feeding organisms.

MUTUALISM is another common relationship in which two species receive benefits from each other. One of the most important examples of this relationship exists between insects and plants. Bees are important **pollinators** of plants. In return, bees receive food from the plants in the form of pollen and nectar.

One of the most interesting interactions between species is known as COMMENSALISM. In commensalism, one species benefits; the other is neither harmed nor helped. Tiny sea anemones are often found growing on the claws of female boxing crabs. Boxing crabs receive protection from the stinging sea anemones by using them as boxing gloves. Apparently, the anemones are not helped or harmed by the relationship. [*See also* BIODIVERSITY; BIOREGION; CONSERVATION; ECOLOGY; ENDANGERED SPECIES; EXTINCTION; and POPULATION GROWTH.]

◆ The use of the ladybird beetle, which feeds on aphids, is an example of biological control of pests.

◆ Releasing natural enemies of insect pests has proven to be an effective biological control method.

themselves against pests. Scientists have also developed methods of interfering with INSECT reproduction. A single biological control method is often less effective than synthetic pesticides. However, results improve when more than one method is used.

PREDATORS

Predators were first used to control agricultural pests more than 100 years ago. In 1888, an insect called the cottony cushion scale had almost destroyed the citrus groves of California. These pests were accidentally imported from Australia. Cottony cushion scales release a sweet, sticky material on lemons and oranges, which encourages the growth of a fungus. The fungus then destroys the fruit. To control the scale insects, farmers imported ladybird beetles, which feed on the pests in Australia. Within a few years, the cottony cushion scales were gone. The Australian ladybird beetle saved the California citrus industry.

Many predatory insects, such as flies, spiders, aphids, and dragonflies, are now used to control agricultural pests. Larger predators such as bats, BIRDS, snakes, and toads are also sometimes used.

PARASITES

Parasites are SPECIES that obtain their nutrients by living on or in other organisms. The parasites most com-monly used as biological controls are parasitic wasps, which kill pests by injecting their eggs into the bodies of the pests. When the young wasps hatch, they feed upon the insides of the pests, killing them in the process.

Parasitic wasps were most successfully used in Africa during the 1980s, when mealybugs and spider mites destroyed nearly 60% of the cassava melon crop. Parasitic wasps were imported from South America, and they brought the pest problem under control.

PATHOGENS

Pathogens, organisms that cause disease, are widely used to limit the pest populations. Farmers might apply BACTERIA, VIRUSES, or FUNGI to weaken or destroy pest populations. The bacterium *Bacillus thuringiensis,* often abbreviated *Bt,* is commonly used to kill the caterpillars of moths and butterflies, as well as other insect **larvae.** GYPSY MOTH caterpillars, which feed on the leaves of trees, can be controlled with *Bt.* Scientists are now trying to develop an INSECTICIDE made from the toxin that *Bt* releases.

One advantage of *Bt* is that it does not harm MAMMALS, birds, or most other organisms. However, applications of *Bt* may kill not only the targeted pest, but also other insects, as well. More research is needed to verify the safety of this method of pest control.

CHEMICALS FROM PLANTS

Many plants produce chemicals to protect themselves from pests. Some of these chemicals have been extracted and are now available as commercial pesticides. Plant chemicals have the advantage of being BIODEGRADABLE, which means that they can be broken down into harmless substances by bacteria and other DECOMPOSERS. Among the more common plant chemicals used are neem oil, pyrethrins, and rotenone.

Biological Diversity
See BIODIVERSITY

Biomagnification
See BIOACCUMULATION

Biomass

▶ The organic matter in PLANTS or plant products that is present in a TROPHIC LEVEL. The biomass in each trophic level is the amount of energy in the form of food or FUEL available to the next trophic level.

The energy at a trophic level can be released when organic matter is burned or broken down by cells in plants, animals, and microorganisms.

◆ At each trophic level, energy is lost as biomass is broken down.

About 90% of the biomass in each trophic level is lost through these kinds of activities and does not reach the next trophic level. Some fuels for heating and for cooling food are referred to as biomass, as well. These fuels include wood, wood chips, bark, and other plant parts. [*See also* ENERGY PYRAMID; FOOD CHAIN; FOOD WEB; FOSSIL FUELS; and GASOHOL.]

◆ Chipped orchard prunings are used as fuel at a Biomass Power Plant in California.

Biome

▶ A major ECOSYSTEM type distinguished by certain PLANTS and animals. Each type of biome has plants and animals that are best adapted to particular CLIMATE conditions, such as amounts and types of PRECIPITATION and temperature ranges. For example, an area with very little precipitation and moderate-to-high temperatures will be a DESERT. An area with very high rainfall and high temperatures will be a tropical RAIN FOREST.

Two regions in very different parts of the world will have plants and animals that have similar ADAPTATIONS if they live in areas that have similar rainfall and average temperatures. Deserts in North America have spiny plants that are part of the cactus family. Deserts in North Africa have spiny plants that are part of the genus **euphorbia**. Although the plants from these two desert areas look similar, they are not closely related. The plants provide an example of CONVERGENT EVOLUTION—they have evolved similar shapes to deal with similar growing conditions.

Animal SPECIES do not necessarily stay within the boundaries of a single biome. For example, some animal species can live in different biomes. In the United States, great horned owls live in the temperate FOREST biome, the desert biome, and the GRASSLAND biome. Other types of animals are restricted to only one biome. The black-footed ferret, for example, is found only in the grassland biome in the western United States.

TYPES OF BIOMES

There are nine main types of terrestrial, or land, biomes. The main types of terrestrial biomes include the TUNDRAS, TAIGAS, temperate forests, GRASSLANDS, SAVANNAS, deserts, temperate rain forests, tropical seasonal forests, and the tropical rain forests.

Tundras

Tundras are biomes that have low temperatures and low precipitation. Low-growing plants, such as sedges, grasses, and low shrubs, are the typical vegetation. Vegetation of the tundra is usually small because of the high winds in the region and the inability of roots to pass through a frozen soil layer called *permafrost*.

Taigas

Taigas have low temperatures and moderate precipitation. Also called boreal forests or CONIFEROUS FORESTS, taigas are dominated by coniferous evergreen trees, such as spruces, firs, hemlocks, and pines.

Temperate Forests

Temperate forests are regions of moderate temperatures and moderate precipitation. A variety of tree species, both deciduous and coniferous, make up dominant plants of the temperate forest. The plants grow in layers, with shrubs, herbs, and mosses growing in the understory and on the forest floor.

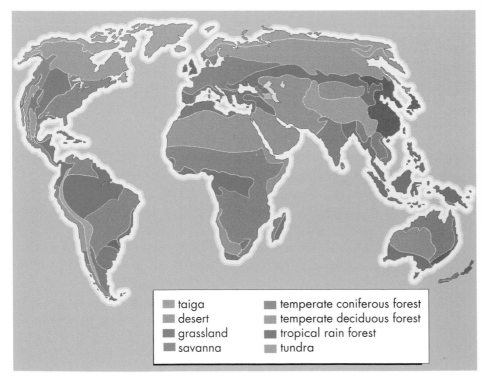

- taiga
- desert
- grassland
- savanna
- temperate coniferous forest
- temperate deciduous forest
- tropical rain forest
- tundra

◆ The map above shows the distribution of major biomes on Earth.

Grasslands

Grasslands have moderate temperatures and low precipitation. The grassland biome is covered with grass species and a wide variety of other **herbaceous** plants. Periodic fire and drought and the GRAZING of large animals such as bison are important in limiting the growth of trees and maintaining the grassland.

Savannas

Savannas have high temperatures and low precipitation. Savannas look like grasslands with scattered trees standing as individuals or in small groups. Savannas usually have three seasons. The seasons are marked by WEATHER conditions that are either cool and dry, hot and dry, or warm and wet.

Deserts

Deserts usually have moderate-to-high temperatures. All deserts have very low precipitation. An area does not need to be hot to be a desert. However, deserts include the world's hottest places. Any area that receives less than approximately 10 inches (25 centimeters) of rainfall each year is a desert. Most deserts occur at about 30° North or South latitude. Sparsely growing plants with protective spines or chemicals are the main vegetation.

Temperate Rain Forests

As the name implies, temperate rain forests develop in areas with moderate temperatures and moder-

◆ Many species of organisms inhabit tropical rain forests.

◆ The desert biome in Arizona is an area with very little rainfall and moderate-to-high temperatures.

ate precipitation. These forests have lush growth, dominated by coniferous trees.

Tropical Seasonal Forests

These forests have high temperatures and moderate precipitation. These forests, located near the equator, have one or two seasons with heavy rain, with a dry season in between.

Tropical Rain Forests

Tropical rain forests have high temperatures and high-to-very-high amounts of precipitation. With abundant water and year-round warm-to-hot weather, tropical rain forests have the greatest **density** and biological diversity of land plants and animals of any biome.

FACTORS THAT AFFECT BIOMES

The temperature and rainfall in an area is partly determined by how far north or south of the equator the area is located. Other characteristics of a location can affect the biomes that develop. Altitude is one of these characteristics. High mountains in the southern United States, for example, often have taiga or tundra biomes at the top, even if the surrounding land is a desert or temperate forest. If you climb a mountain in the western United States, you could start off in a desert, hike through a temperate forest, then walk through a taiga, and finally end up in a tundra biome at the top of the mountain. [*See also* BIOREGION; CLIMATE CHANGE; and DESERTIFICATION.]

Biophilia

◗ A controversial hypothesis espoused by biologist Edward Osborne WILSON that humans have developed an evolutionary need for nature. The word *biophilia* literally means "love of life." According to Wilson's biophilia hypothesis, humans have an innate tendency to focus on living things and life processes, and this focus affects human decisions.

◆ Visitors to Kenya, as well as residents, may be awed by scenes such as this sunrise over Masai-Mara.

◆ A love of animals and a fascination with the workings of nature often appear to be innate human attributes.

◆ Humans show a need for relationships with other living things.

Many scientists view the SAVANNA of eastern Africa as the probable evolutionary origin of modern human populations. As an example of his hypothesis, Wilson notes that humans who have settled in many different parts of the world have created landscapes (such as lawns, gardens, and parks) that resemble the African savanna, even in densely populated urban areas. Wilson believes the need of humans to conserve nature goes beyond the need for food and shelter. He also believes it includes a need to be linked to nature. Wilson interprets our need for relationships with other SPECIES, such as pets and PLANTS, as evidence of biophilia. [*See also* BIODIVERSITY and EVOLUTION.]

Bioregion

▶A large, intact, and continuous ECOSYSTEM that shares common characteristics and may extend across the borders of different cities, states, or even countries. Many ecologists use the bioregion as the basis for preserving ecosystems. An ecosystem may be identified by its organisms, SOIL, CLIMATE, topography (hills, valleys, and so on), geology, and its water (how much and in what form it occurs). The contiguous, or connecting, land area in which these characteristics are the same make up a bioregion.

Bioregions rely on nature's boundaries rather than on political boundaries. For example, a river may form the border of two countries. Yet the land on either side of the river may be part of a single bioregion. Thus, if scientists seek to protect a threatened organism in this ecosystem, the entire bioregion must be preserved. In this example, this task would involve the cooperation of the two countries whose borders are on the river.

LIVING WITHIN THE BIOREGION

Bioregionalism is used by many as a nontechnical, nonscientific means to describe a way of living that conforms to the region in which people live. According to this view, people should try to eat foods grown in their region. They should also try to use wood native to their region and cultivate gardens using PLANTS that are native to the area.

NATIVE SPECIES of plants are more likely to survive in the area and require fewer PESTICIDES and fertilizers than do EXOTIC SPECIES, which are alien to the region. Furthermore, through the purchase of locally grown food, money is saved and AIR POLLUTION is reduced, because the crops did not have to be hauled across the country by truck. Supporters of bioregionalism state that conforming a lifestyle to the resources in one's ecosystem not only makes environmental sense but gives one a sense of rootedness in the community. It also helps develop a sensitivity to the ENVIRONMENT. [*See also* BIOME; ECOLOGICAL ECONOMICS; and LAND USE.]

Bioremediation

▶The use of microbes, such as BACTERIA and some FUNGI, to break down pollutants into less toxic substances. Microbes have always consumed and broken down some human wastes, such as SEWAGE. Bioremediation involves the use of microbes to break down pollutants, including oil, PESTICIDES, and TOXIC WASTES such as cyanides and chlorinated HYDROCARBONS.

There are many methods of bioremediation. Some use microbes that already exist in nature. Others use microbes modified by GENETIC ENGINEERING to do a certain job. A genetically engineered bacterium that helps to clean up OIL SPILLS has been in use since 1990. This bacterium destroys spilled oil instead

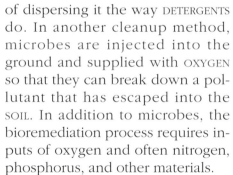

◆ Oil spill.

◆ Composting.

of dispersing it the way DETERGENTS do. In another cleanup method, microbes are injected into the ground and supplied with OXYGEN so that they can break down a pollutant that has escaped into the SOIL. In addition to microbes, the bioremediation process requires inputs of oxygen and often nitrogen, phosphorus, and other materials.

There are limits to bioremediation. It cannot be used to clean up all types of toxic spills and wastes. It is also important to avoid using microbes that cause new problems while solving old ones. Still, bioremediation is useful, and further research is likely to produce new ways of fighting POLLUTION with microorganisms. [*See also* BIODEGRADABLE; DECOMPOSITION; EXXON VALDEZ; GARBAGE; HAZARDOUS WASTES; and SUPERFUND.]

◆ Sewage treatment plant.

Biosphere

D The portion of Earth from the ocean depths to the upper ATMOSPHERE that contains life. The word *biosphere* comes from the Greek word *bios,* meaning "life," and the Latin word *sphaera,* which means "total range." Thus, the biosphere contains every living SPECIES on Earth. It is the largest possible BIOLOGICAL COMMUNITY.

Compared to the total size of Earth, the biosphere is small. Most organisms exist only in the lower portion of the atmosphere to about 5 miles (8 kilometers) above Earth's surface, at and below the surface (the LITHOSPHERE), and within bodies of water (the HYDROSPHERE) or the SEDIMENTS below bodies of water. Exceptions include spores and microscopic organisms that are carried by air currents high into the atmosphere. Recent discoveries of rare species of BACTERIA that live deep within Earth in oil reservoirs have also surprised scientists. The biosphere provides organisms with all the nutrients and resources they need to survive. These resources include food, water, OXYGEN, sunlight, and shelter.

Scientists have identified and studied about 1.5 million different species of organisms living in the biosphere. Each year, many new organisms are added to the list. However, most scientists believe that people have only "scratched the surface" in the quest to identify the diversity of life in the biosphere. Thus, it is likely that only a fraction of the actual number of living organisms on Earth has been discovered and studied.

Earth's biosphere can be divided into a number of large biological communities called BIOMES. Biomes are regions of Earth with distinct CLIMATES and organisms. Examples of biomes are DESERTS, GRASSLANDS, and tropical RAIN FORESTS.

Biomes can be divided into several types of ECOSYSTEMS. Within ecosystems, organisms interact with each other and with their physical

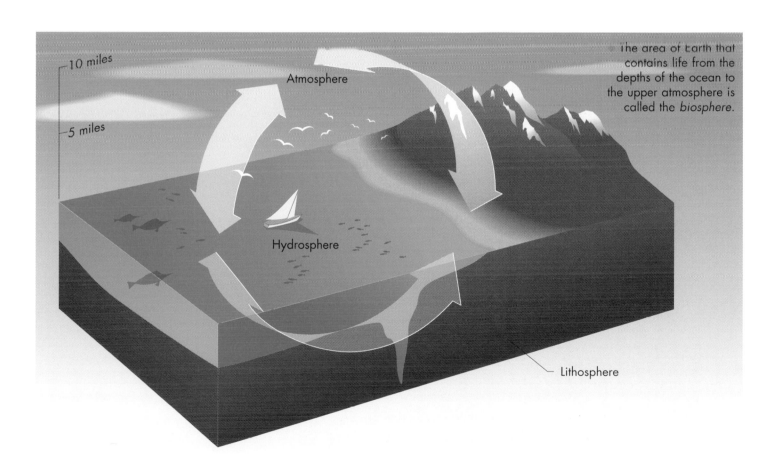

The area of Earth that contains life from the depths of the ocean to the upper atmosphere is called the *biosphere.*

ENVIRONMENT in a variety of ways. For example, organisms interact with each other through predation, COMPETITION, PARASITISM, MUTUALISM, and COMMENSALISM. These relationships help organisms obtain the energy needed to fuel their life processes. Such relationships allow organisms to interact with their physical environment as they help circulate matter, such as water, oxygen, nitrogen, and CARBON, through the ecosystem.

Humans, too, are part of the biosphere. However, many human activities have had a negative impact on the biosphere. The illegal dumping of wastes into oceans and other bodies of water, the burning of FOSSIL FUELS, and the large-scale MINING of MINERALS and other resources such as COAL, have led to POLLUTION of the air, land, and sea. Today, many people feel that we must conserve the biosphere's resources and coexist peacefully with other organisms to ensure the health and success of future generations. [*See also* BIO-GEOCHEMICAL CYCLE; CLIMAX COMMUNITY; CONSERVATION; ECOLOGY; GAIA HYPOTHESIS; and POLLUTION.]

◆ From left to right: Chestnut mandibled toucan, warbler finch, bald eagle (at bottom), and the magnificent frigate bird.

no other animals besides birds have feathers.

Birds are members of the group of animals called VERTEBRATES, which also includes FISH, MAMMALS, REPTILES, and AMPHIBIANS. Vertebrates are animals with a backbone.

About 8,600 SPECIES of birds exist today. Birds range in size from the tiny hummingbird, which weighs less than 35 ounces (992 grams) to the ostrich, which weighs more than 275 pounds (125 kilograms). Birds live in almost every kind of ENVIRONMENT on Earth—FORESTS, GRASSLANDS, DESERTS, mountains, the ARCTIC and ANTARCTICA, on farms, and in cities. The first known bird, called *Archaeopteryx*, appeared about 140 million years ago. It probably evolved from a species of small tree-climbing dinosaurs that leaped from branch to branch.

Bird

▶ An animal that lays hard-shelled eggs and has feathers and wings. Most birds are able to fly, though some cannot. The ability to fly is not unique to birds, since bats and some INSECTS can also fly. However,

◆ Somali ostrich.

◆ American robin.

◆ Mature bald eagle.

◆ Broad-billed hummingbird, male.

◆ Brown pelican.

The skeletons of modern birds are well adapted for flight. The bones are thin and hollow, which decreases the weight that the bird must lift in the air. The sternum (breastbone) is large, which provides a sturdy anchor for the large muscles used for flying.

Many birds have complex behavioral ADAPTATIONS. Their courtship and mating rituals are elaborate, and they devote much energy to incubating their eggs and caring for their young. Most birds migrate away from their mating and nesting HABITAT each year to their winter habitats in warmer climates. One species of bird, the arctic tern, has the longest migratory route of any living animal. It travels 22,000 miles (35,000 kilometers) roundtrip each year.

BIRDS IN ECOSYSTEMS

Birds, like all living things, have important roles in their ECOSYSTEMS. They are food for other animals, including snakes, foxes, and raccoons. They prey on organisms, especially insects and earthworms, keeping them from becoming too numerous. Some birds help farmers by eating agricultural pests. For example, sparrows and robins eat tomato worms and cabbageworms. Hawks and owls prey upon animals such as rats and rabbits, which eat stored grain. Other birds eat the seeds of weeds, helping to keep the weeds on farmland under control.

Some birds help PLANTS reproduce. Hummingbirds, for instance, pollinate flowers. As they move among flowers, feeding on nectar, they carry the pollen picked up from one plant to other plants nearby. Other birds help plants reproduce by spreading their seeds. After they eat the fruits of plants, the birds pass the seeds in their droppings. The seeds may then sprout where they were dropped, sometimes far from where the original plants grew.

EXTINCT AND ENDANGERED BIRDS

At least 80 species of birds have become extinct within the last 300 years. Most of them became extinct because of human activity. The dodos, for example, were large flightless birds that became extinct after sailors hunted them for food. PASSENGER PIGEONS were also hunted to EXTINCTION.

Today, HABITAT LOSS, rather than HUNTING, is the major cause of bird extinctions. A species' habitat may be destroyed by the clearing of land, the construction of buildings and roads, or POLLUTION. The number of whooping cranes in North America was reduced to only 33 birds in the 1930s, mainly because of habitat destruction. Since then, conservationists have made a concerted effort to protect whooping cranes, and their numbers have risen to more than 230 birds. Other birds in the United States that are threatened or endangered include BALD EAGLES, CALIFORNIA CONDORS, and ospreys. [*See also* ENDANGERED SPECIES; ENDANGERED SPECIES ACT; MIGRATION; POLLINATION; WILDLIFE; and WILDLIFE CONSERVATION.]

Bonneville Power Administration (BPA)

Independent agency created to control the sale and distribution of electric power generated primarily by the hydroelectric DAMS of the Columbia and Snake river systems. The construction of dams for generating HYDROELECTRIC POWER began in the 1930s in the Columbia Basin. The first dam completed along the rivers was at Bonneville, and the agency took its name from this project. Dozens of dams were built for electric power generation, navigation, flood control, and IRRIGATION in the Columbia and Snake river basins.

As the broker for ELECTRICITY in most of Washington, Oregon, Idaho, and Montana, BPA plays a major role in decisions regarding electric power sales throughout the region. Major industries, especially the ALUMINUM industry, were attracted by the abundant and inexpensive supply of electricity in the area. By the late 1970s, every potential dam site in the Columbia and Snake basins had been developed, with the exception of an area near HANFORD, WASHINGTON, a major site for research and development of NUCLEAR WEAPONS and NUCLEAR POWER. The building of dams caused a decline in SALMON. Today measures are being taken to save the endangered salmon. Because of the effect of such measures on the amount of electricity that will be available for BPA to sell, the

◆ The building of dams can result in the decline of salmon populations.

agency, along with other agencies like the National Marine Fisheries Service, the Northwest Power Planning Council, and tribal fisheries managers, has been directly involved in the measures taken to save the endangered salmon. [*See also* ENDANGERED SPECIES; WATER, DRINKING; and WATERSHED.]

reactor. For every four atoms of PLUTONIUM used in the reactor, five new atoms of plutonium are formed from the uranium-238, which is why it is called breeder.

Breeder reactors are attractive because URANIUM supplies are

limited. Breeder reactors can be fueled by U-238, a waste product of uranium processing plants, or spent fuel from nuclear fission reactors. In addition to providing a long-lasting supply of ELECTRICITY, breeder reactors could reduce the need for the MINING and processing of uranium ore. In the United States, the estimated supply of fuel for breeder reactors would last 1,000 years or more. The downside of this technology is that it takes about 30 years for the reactor to produce as much P-239 as the fuel it consumes; it also produces NUCLEAR WASTE. [*See also* NUCLEAR FUSION and NUCLEAR POWER.]

Breeder Reactor

▶ A type of nuclear reactor that generates new FUEL as it produces heat energy. Neutrons from the NUCLEAR FISSION change stable atoms of abundant uranium-238 (U-238) into an unstable isotope, plutonium-239 (P-239). P-239 can then be used as a nuclear fuel in the

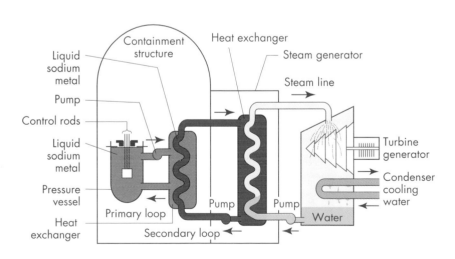

◆ In a breeder reactor, energy to produce electricity is produced as well as more fuel in the form of plutonium-239.

Bureau of Land Management

U.S. DEPARTMENT OF THE INTERIOR
BUREAU OF LAND MANAGEMENT

▶A federal agency of the United States under the DEPARTMENT OF THE INTERIOR that manages more than 270 million acres (108 million hectares) of PUBLIC LAND and the resources on them. Its stated philosophy is that management is "based on the principles of multiple use and sustained yield." However, the way it manages FORESTS, RANGELANDS, and WILDERNESS has inspired bitter debate. Many people are critical of its policy of charging nominal fees for grazing rights to vast tracts of public land. In 1990, a typical year, the cost of administering the grazing-rights program amounted to $50 million, but income from the leases amounted to only $19 million. Also, many experts believe that public lands are damaged by the great numbers of LIVESTOCK permitted to graze on them. [*See also* CATTLE; GRASSLANDS; and OVERGRAZING.]

Bureau of Reclamation

▶An agency of the federal government that manages water resources in the western United States. The Bureau of Reclamation was established in 1902 as part of the DEPARTMENT OF THE INTERIOR. The job of the bureau is to develop the water resources of the western states, an area where fresh water is a scarce NATURAL RESOURCE.

CONSTRUCTION PROJECTS

The Bureau of Reclamation was given the task of building 600 DAMS and 53,000 miles (85,800 kilometers) of canals to supply water to the farmers who occupied most of the land in the western United States. The Hoover Dam on the Colorado River, which was completed in 1936, is an example. It was built to provide flood control, HYDROELECTRIC POWER, drinking water, and IRRIGATION water. Lake Mead, the RESERVOIR behind the

◆ The use of water for farm irrigation in the United States is a concern of the Bureau of Reclamation.

dam, is a recreation area that also supplies water to Las Vegas and parts of California.

In 1985, the Central Arizona Project, funded by $3.9 billion of federal taxes, began pumping water from the Colorado River to the cities of Phoenix and Tucson, in Arizona. Southern California immediately lost about one-fifth of its water supply, which is diverted from the river through the Colorado River Aqueduct. As a result of such problems, reclamation projects have become increasingly controversial. This controversy led the bureau in 1987 to announce that it would plan no more large-scale construction projects.

WATER RIGHTS

The Bureau of Reclamation controls the WATER RIGHTS to most of the water in the western United States. Few people are happy with this system. Farmers are supplied with water at highly subsidized prices, whereas others suffer water shortages. The problem can be traced to laws that treat water differently from other commodities. For example, water in streams and lakes is not privately owned; only the rights to use it are owned. This system has several flaws when applied to dry areas.

1. CONSERVATION may save WETLANDS but lose all the water in them. Organizations sometimes buy wetlands to preserve the HABITAT of water BIRDS. However, they also need to buy rights to the wetland's water, which the Bureau of Reclamation may choose not to sell.

For instance, California's Central Valley is part of the Pacific Flyway, one of the four "flight lanes" used by millions of birds as they travel between their northern nesting grounds and southern wintering regions. The birds stop in wetlands during their MIGRATION. In 1970, more than 10 million ducks wintered in the Central Valley. By 1985, so much water had been diverted to agriculture from valley wetlands that the number had fallen to less than 2 million.

2. Farmers have to use up all the water allotted to them. If farmers do not use all the water they are allotted in one year, the bureau can allow them less water the following year. Thus, farmers have no incentive to conserve water. More than 50% of irrigation water is wasted by evaporation and leakage. In 20 years, Israel has doubled the amount of food it can produce using one acre-foot of water. Unlike farmers in the United States, farmers in Israel practice aggressive water conservation.

3. Owners cannot transfer water rights without permission from the Bureau of Reclamation. In 1989, a Nevada water company agreed to sell Colorado River water that it

did not need to the Las Vegas suburb of Henderson, Nevada. Bureau lawyers stopped the sale. Thus, a farmer who pays the bureau $5 per acre-foot of water usually cannot get permission to sell that water to a town that would be happy to pay $500 for it.

PROGRESS ON WESTERN WATER RIGHTS

The rules that cover water rights are slowly changing. Cities such as Tucson and Phoenix in Arizona and Albuquerque in New Mexico now buy water rights from nearby farmers for up to $2,000 per acre-foot. Since about 1988, the bureau has permitted water to be sold from agricultural areas to sites in California.

In 1992, the rules for California's Central Valley Project (CVP) were also changed. The CVP controls about one-fifth of California's water. For the past 50 years, it has sold 90% of its water cheaply to farmers, while cities, industries, and the ENVIRONMENT suffered from water shortages. The business community rebelled, arguing that California, had little chance of economic growth as long as industries could not move into southern California, and towns could not expand because of the lack of water. Over the objections of Congressional representatives from Central Valley, Congress voted overwhelmingly to allot more CVP water to towns and to WILDLIFE habitats such as rivers and wetlands. [*See also* WATER, DRINKING and WATER RIGHTS.]

C

California Condor

▶ An extremely rare **vulture** of the western United States that is in danger of EXTINCTION. The California condor, *Gymnogyps californianus,* is classified in the same family of BIRDS as vultures, buzzards, and Andean condors. This large bird once soared freely across the skies of the western United States from southern California to Oregon. Today, the California condor is nearly extinct—only about 60 exist, mostly in captivity.

The California condor is the largest flying land bird in North America. It has an average wing-span of 9 feet (3 meters), a body length of about 50 inches (127 centimeters), and a weight of up to 31 pounds (14 kilograms). The adult California condor is very recognizable. Most of this large bird's body is covered by black feathers. White feathers cover the undersides of its wings. A ruff of black feathers encircles the base of the California condor's neck, which is featherless and has the same red-orange color as the bird's head.

HABITAT AND NICHE

In the wild, condors live in mountainous areas, where they spend much of their time resting on high cliffs. Unlike most birds, condors do not build nests. They lay their eggs in caves and holes or among rocks high on mountain ledges. A female California condor lays just one egg every two years.

Condors are powerful fliers. They may flap their wings only about once per hour as they glide across vast expanses of territory, searching the ground below for food. Like other vultures, condors eat carrion—the remains of dead animals. Thus, condors are classified as scavengers.

THREATS TO THE CALIFORNIA CONDOR

The California condor was once widespread in the Western United States. However, by 1984, only about 20 of the birds remained in the wild. The decline of the condor is largely the result of human activities, such as HUNTING, construction that results in HABITAT LOSS for the condors, and side effects resulting from the use of the insecticide dichlorodiphenyl trichloroethane, (DDT).

Hunting

Many condors were killed by the direct or indirect actions of hunters.

◆ The California condor is an extremely rare vulture that lives in the Western Hemisphere.

◆ In 1992, scientists began releasing condors raised in captivity.

In some cases, hunters shot and killed condors in the mistaken belief that they spread disease. In other cases, condors died from LEAD poisoning that resulted from eating the remains of animals that had been shot with lead bullets. Ranchers unintentionally brought about the deaths of even more condors. These accidental deaths resulted from attempts made by ranchers to kill coyotes and other PREDATORS suspected of attacking their herds and flocks. Many condors died from eating animal carcasses that contained poisons set out by ranchers.

Habitat Loss

The survival of the California condor has been severely threatened by habitat loss. As the human population in the U.S. western coastal states grew, cities that spread out in all directions developed. The condor's way of life requires vast areas of flying space over open, mountainous areas. The building of homes and offices in these areas has destroyed, or altered, much of the natural ENVIRONMENT in mountain regions. As a result, the HABITAT of the condor has been lost.

Insecticides

DDT is a synthetic insecticide that was abundantly used in the mid-twentieth century. DDT was used to kill INSECTS that carried diseases such as malaria, yellow fever, and typhus. Unfortunately, DDT also had some unwanted characteristics. It remains in the environment for years after its initial use. In addition, through a process called BIOACCUMULATION, DDT collects in the tissues of organisms and increases in concentration as it moves through some FOOD CHAINS. Through bioaccumulation, high concentrations of DDT build up in the tissues of some FISH and birds, including the California condor.

THE LANGUAGE OF THE ENVIRONMENT

embryo early stage of an animal's development.

vulture a large bird, usually with a naked head, that feeds on the decaying flesh of dead animals.

The DDT that accumulated in the tissues of the condors did not poison the birds. However, in the 1970s, it was discovered that the DDT caused the eggs of the infected condor to become thin and fragile. This problem caused the eggs to break before the chick **embryo** inside had fully developed. With few new birds hatching to replace those that died, the condor population dwindled further.

After years of study, the United States finally banned the use of DDT in 1972. However, because DDT remained in the environment for a long time, its effect continued to plague the condor.

SAVING THE CALIFORNIA CONDOR

Many scientists have worked to try to prevent the extinction of the California condor. Some of the most successful efforts in the crusade have involved the use of CAPTIVE PROPAGATION. In 1982, biologists set out to capture all California condors left in the wild. The last wild condor was snared in 1987. Since then, more than 35 condors have been hatched and raised in controlled surroundings.

The raising of baby California condors has involved some unusual methods. To aid in the feeding of young condors, some zoo workers wore hand puppets that resembled the head of a female California condor. The workers discovered that the baby birds quickly adapted to taking nourishment from the mouth of the "mother" puppet, which helped more of the hatchlings survive in captivity.

The raising of California condors in captivity has met with some success. In 1992, scientists began releasing some of the zoo-raised condors into the wild. Although the California condor remains on the ENDANGERED SPECIES list and is thus protected, some of the released birds have already died as a result of illegal hunting.

Cancer

▶A disease characterized by the rapid, irregular growth of cells. Cancer can be deadly because it spreads easily to many parts of the body. The many forms of cancer are classified into four groups: carcinomas—cancers of the skin, a gland, or lining of an organ; sarcomas—cancers of the bones and muscles; leukemia—cancers involving white blood cells; and lymphomas—cancers of the body's lymphatic system. The lymphatic system carries the fluids that bathe cells through the body.

Hippocrates (ca. 460–ca. 377 B.C.), the Greek physician generally regarded as the father of medicine, coined the term *carcinoma*. The term comes from the Greek word meaning "crab." Scientists have discovered cancers in most multicellular animals. They have even discovered cancers in dinosaur bones and in Egyptian mummies. Today, cancer is one of the leading causes of death in the United States. The most common cancers are those of the skin, lungs, colon, breasts, and prostate.

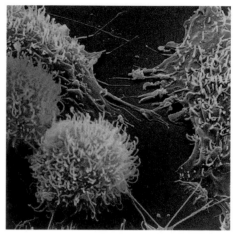

◆ Cancer cells divide more rapidly than normal cells.

CAUSES OF CANCER

The causes of cancer are difficult to identify. Scientists believe environmental, biological, and genetic factors may be involved. Cancer begins when a CARCINOGEN, or cancer-causing agent, causes mutations, or changes, in a cell's GENES. Genes are parts of chromosomes that carry the instructions that direct cell processes. When genes mutate malignantly, abnormal cells form. These abnormal cells reproduce rapidly, forming a mass of cells known as a *tumor*. When tumors spread to other parts of the body, they can crowd out and destroy normal cells, robbing them of essential nutrients.

Scientists have identified a variety of cancer-causing agents. Chemicals found in smoke and AIR POLLUTION, ASBESTOS, and certain forms of RADIATION are some of the known carcinogens in the ENVIRONMENT. Evidence supporting the belief that environmental factors cause cancer is found by observing

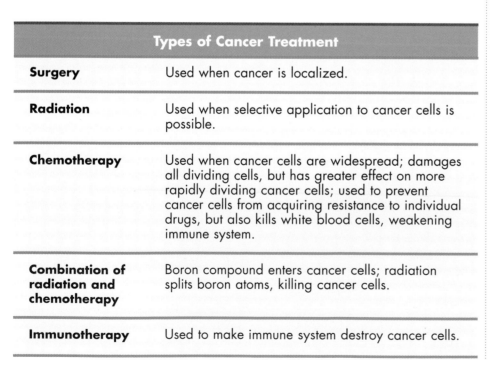

Types of Cancer Treatment	
Surgery	Used when cancer is localized.
Radiation	Used when selective application to cancer cells is possible.
Chemotherapy	Used when cancer cells are widespread; damages all dividing cells, but has greater effect on more rapidly dividing cancer cells; used to prevent cancer cells from acquiring resistance to individual drugs, but also kills white blood cells, weakening immune system.
Combination of radiation and chemotherapy	Boron compound enters cancer cells; radiation splits boron atoms, killing cancer cells.
Immunotherapy	Used to make immune system destroy cancer cells.

◆ Scientists warn that prolonged, unprotected exposure to radiation from the sun can cause skin cancer.

that people in different countries get different types of cancer at different rates. For instance, breast cancer is common in the United States, but relatively rare in Japan. Similarly, stomach cancer is common in China, but relatively rare in the United States. Scientists use these types of patterns to pinpoint carcinogens in the environment.

TREATMENT FOR CANCER

Many cancers can be treated in a variety of ways. Most cancer treatments involve surgery, chemotherapy, and treatment with radiation. Surgery is often the first step in treatment if it has been determined that a tumor is restricted to a particular body part and has not spread. If cancerous cells have spread, radiation and chemotherapy are the

most common treatments. These methods involve treating the affected parts of the body with radiation or chemicals to destroy the cancerous cells. Once most of the cancer cells are destroyed, the body's immune system, the body system that defends the body against disease, can take over and kill any remaining cells. Unfortunately, both radiation and chemotherapy treatments can produce unpleasant side effects in the patient, including nausea, dizziness, and other flu-like symptoms, as well as weight loss and hair loss.

Scientists constantly seek new cancer treatments as well as a cure for cancer. Cancer researchers are particularly interested in the genetic causes of cancer. Scientists have already identified many cancer-causing genes in the body, includ-

ing genes involved in breast and colon cancer. Eventually, using the tools of GENETIC ENGINEERING, scientists hope to replace defective genes with normal ones. [*See also* OZONE HOLE; PCBS; and ULTRAVIOLET RADIATION.]

Captive Propagation

▶The controlled mating and breeding of animals and PLANTS in ZOOS, aquariums, and botanical gardens. Captive-breeding programs are especially useful for increasing the numbers of critically endangered or threatened SPECIES. Several species in the United States, such as the CALIFORNIA CONDOR, black-footed ferret, and whooping crane, have benefited from captive-breeding programs. As a result, these species' numbers continue to grow.

In some cases, captive-propagation programs allow endangered populations to increase enough so that the species can be reintroduced into the wild. In the early 1970s, an animal known as the Arabian oryx barely escaped EXTINCTION after being overhunted in the DESERTS of the Middle East. The species was placed in a captive-breeding program and is now gradually being returned to the wild.

While captive propagation has helped some species, it does have several disadvantages. In addition to being expensive, captive-breeding programs are time-consuming. Con-

◆ The Arabian oryx was driven to near-extinction in the 1970s. Captive breeding of this species has been successful. The Arabian oryx now breeds in the wild, but it remains endangered.

sequently, hundreds of critically ENDANGERED SPECIES move closer to extinction while "waiting in line" for a program. Also, animals often get sick or won't breed in captivity. On balance, however, captive-breeding programs are viewed as quite successful, because they play an important role in most endangered species recovery plans. [*See also* CONSERVATION and WILDLIFE.]

Carbon

◗ A nonmetallic chemical element that makes up less than .03% of Earth's crust but is one of Earth's most important elements. Carbon is the base of all organic molecules that make up living or once-living things.

Graphite and diamond are pure forms of carbon. However, most carbon exists in combination with other elements to form substances such as CARBON DIOXIDE and calcium carbonate (limestone). There are approximately 1 million known carbon **compounds.** The most plentiful exist in organisms as carbohydrates, which are compounds of carbon, hydrogen, and OXYGEN. All living things need carbon to exist. In fact, there are millions of carbon atoms in every cell of your body and those of other organisms. Besides being part of your body structure, carbohydrates are present in foods (sugars and starches) and fiber. These substances supply your body with an energy source. Nutritionists believe that as much as 60% of your daily diet should consist of carbohydrates.

Many manufactured products contain some form of carbon. In addition, carbon compounds are commonly given off as wastes of industrial activities. Carbon black,

or amorphous carbon, is a black powder **residue** that results from the partial heating or burning of carbon-containing materials. For example, when oil, NATURAL GAS, or COAL is burned without enough oxygen, it leaves a fine black soot of carbon black. This soot is used to make paint and rubber products.

Animal or bone charcoal and carbon-containing wood charcoal are produced by burning wood without a sufficient air supply to entirely consume the wood. Charcoal is used as cooking fuel and in products to filter odors and impurities from air and water. Charcoal-filtering is used in fish-tank filters to keep the water clean. Tiny tubes inside some medicine bottles or tape-player cartons contain carbon that is used to keep impurities from contaminating the contents.

CARBON AND THE ENVIRONMENT

Carbon dioxide is a waste gas given off by almost all living things. It also results from the burning of FOSSIL FUELS, tropical DEFORESTATION, and DECOMPOSITION. As fossil fuels such as coal and oil are burned, they release carbon dioxide. Trees and other plants use carbon dioxide from the air to carry out PHOTOSYNTHESIS. As trees are cut down or burned out of an area, they can no longer absorb carbon dioxide. Instead, they give off carbon dioxide as they are burned or as they decay.

Carbon dioxide is one of the GREENHOUSE GASES, along with METHANE, CFCS, and NITROGEN OXIDE. Scientists believe a buildup of

◆ Graphite is pure carbon in its softest form.

◆ Diamond, the hardest known substance, is also pure carbon.

these gases in the ATMOSPHERE may result in GLOBAL WARMING. In our atmosphere, the greenhouse gases act like a greenhouse by trapping heat near Earth's surface. The gases allow the sun's light to reach Earth but prevent Earth's heat from being released into space. Although it is not proven, some scientists believe that an accumulation of greenhouse gases in the atmosphere may be causing average temperatures worldwide to rise.

According to *The Environmental Sourcebook* by Edith C. Stein, the United States is responsible for approximately 25% of the world's emissions of carbon dioxide from fossil fuels. Electric power plants account for the largest amount of carbon dioxide emitted into the air (35%), followed by transportation (30%), manufacturing (25%), and homes and businesses (10%). Conservationists encourage businesses and individuals to begin searching for and using ALTERNATIVE ENERGY SOURCES and to increase their ENERGY EFFICIENCY so the buildup of carbon dioxide and other greenhouse gases in our atmosphere can be slowed. [*See also* ENVIRONMENTAL ETHICS; GREENHOUSE EFFECT; HEALTH AND NUTRITION; and HYDROCARBONS.]

Carbon Cycle

▶The process by which CARBON is cycled within an ECOSYSTEM. Carbon, as well as water, nitrogen, OXYGEN, and phosphorous, is an essential nutrient for living organisms. Like these other substances, carbon is continuously cycled between organisms and the ENVIRONMENT.

Carbon exists in pure form, as diamond and graphite. It also exists as compounds in the environment and in the cells and tissues of organisms. One compound of carbon is CARBON DIOXIDE (CO_2) gas present in the ATMOSPHERE and in OCEANS and other bodies of water. From the atmosphere, carbon moves into terrestrial and aquatic ecosystems, where it is absorbed by PLANTS, ALGAE, and other PRODUCERS. These organisms use carbon dioxide to carry out PHOTOSYNTHESIS— the food-making activity of producers. During photosynthesis, carbon dioxide, water, and energy from the sun react to form carbon-containing, energy-rich sugars that are stored by the producer. Animals, BACTERIA, FUNGI, and other CONSUMERS obtain this carbon when they feed upon producers or consumers that have eaten producers.

Animals, plants, and other organisms help return carbon to the environment during cellular RESPIRATION—the energy-making process of cells. As food is broken down and used by cells, carbon dioxide gas is formed and released into Earth's atmosphere.

HUMAN ACTIVITY AND THE CARBON CYCLE

Like most organisms, humans help return carbon to the environment during cellular respiration. However, humans also interfere with the

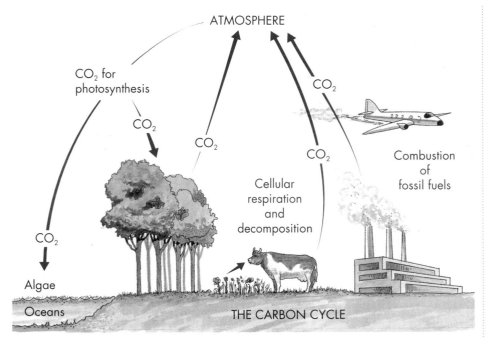

ATMOSPHERE

CO₂ for photosynthesis

CO₂

CO₂

CO₂

CO₂

CO₂

Cellular respiration and decomposition

Combustion of fossil fuels

Algae

Oceans

THE CARBON CYCLE

◆ The carbon cycle. Carbon moves into the food chain and then out into the physical environment. Human activities also contribute to the carbon cycle.

natural cycling of carbon whenever wood FOSSIL FUELS are burned for energy. When factories, AUTOMOBILES, and power plants use fossil fuels for energy, carbon dioxide is added to the atmosphere as a waste product.

Many scientists believe excess carbon dioxide in the atmosphere can have negative effects on the environment. For example, carbon dioxide is a GREENHOUSE GAS. As a greenhouse gas, carbon dioxide traps heat near Earth's surface, causing a phenomenon known as the GREENHOUSE EFFECT. Scientists are concerned that too much carbon dioxide in the atmosphere may also cause GLOBAL WARMING, which could have a devastating effect on all ecosystems. [*See also* BIOGEOCHEMICHAL CYCLE; CHEMICAL CYCLES; and DEFORESTATION.]

Carbon Dioxide

▶ A colorless, odorless, nonpoisonous gas that is a by-product of FOSSIL FUEL use and the energy-making process of organisms. PLANTS and other photosynthetic organisms, such as ALGAE and some species of BACTERIA, use carbon dioxide (CO_2) to make food in the process of PHOTOSYNTHESIS.

CARBON DIOXIDE CYCLING IN ECOSYSTEMS

Organisms are composed primarily of chemical compounds that contain the element CARBON. Life could not exist without this critical chemical. Carbon enters ECOSYSTEMS when plants, algae, and other PRODUCERS

take in carbon dioxide from the ATMOSPHERE for use during photosynthesis. In this chemical reaction, producers use the energy of sunlight to change water and carbon dioxide into food and OXYGEN gas. Animals, FUNGI, and other CONSUMERS obtain carbon through the FOOD CHAIN by feeding on plants, or by eating other consumers.

Carbon dioxide cycles back into the atmosphere in two different ways. All organisms need energy to carry out their biological processes. When organisms burn food through the process of cellular RESPIRATION to make energy, carbon dioxide is released as a waste product. Carbon dioxide is also released when wood is burned and when motor vehicles, factories, and power plants burn COAL, oil, NATURAL GAS, and other fossil fuels to make energy.

CARBON DIOXIDE AND GLOBAL WARMING

Carbon dioxide gas exists in small amounts in the atmosphere, making up less than 1% of all atmospheric gases. However, scientists today are concerned that the amount of carbon dioxide in the air is increasing. Through a study that began in 1958 by geochemist Charles Keeling, scientists have shown that atmospheric levels of carbon dioxide increased by 12% over a 26-year period.

Where is the extra carbon dioxide coming from? Plants and other producers use only some of the carbon dioxide they take in from the atmosphere for photosynthesis. Some of the carbon in the carbon dioxide becomes part of the organ-

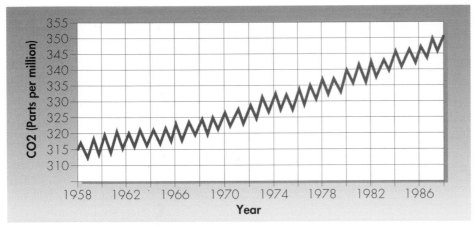

The graph shows the increase of carbon dioxide in the atmosphere from 1958 to 1994.

Carbon monoxide is released from gasoline powered vehicles and contributes to air pollution.

ism. This carbon will stay inside the plant until it dies and decays. Some plants, however, never completely decay. Instead, they are slowly buried by sand, mud, and silt. After millions of years underground, they are changed in form and become fossil fuels—oil, coal, and gas. Each year, millions of tons of carbon dioxide are released into the atmosphere when these fossil fuels are burned for energy.

The burning of living plants also releases carbon dioxide. When tropical RAIN FORESTS are burned to clear land for agriculture, atmospheric levels of carbon dioxide increase.

Environmentalists are concerned about the rise of carbon dioxide levels because of its role as a GREENHOUSE GAS, a gas that contributes to the GREENHOUSE EFFECT. Carbon dioxide, chlorofluorocarbons (CFCS), METHANE, NITROUS OXIDES, and other greenhouse gases cause the greenhouse effect by trapping heat near Earth's surface.

Many scientists believe that the greenhouse effect has resulted in GLOBAL WARMING, a gradual increase in the average world temperature. Environmentalists fear global warming because of its potential effects on weather patterns. Altered weather patterns resulting from a warmer Earth can have serious consequences for ecosystems because all organisms are adapted to survive within particular temperature ranges. [*See also* CARBON CYCLE; CLIMATE; and DEFORESTATION.]

Carbon Monoxide

DA colorless, odorless, poisonous gas. Carbon monoxide is a compound made up of one atom of CARBON and one atom of OXYGEN. The chemical formula for carbon monoxide is CO.

For a substance to burn completely, an adequate oxygen supply must be present. Carbon monoxide is a gas that forms when carbon compounds are burned in an ENVIRONMENT that does not contain enough oxygen. It often forms from the burning of gasoline in AUTOMOBILES, from the burning of oil, COAL, or wood in home heating systems, and from the burning of tobacco in cigarettes.

When carbon monoxide is taken into the lungs during breathing, it is picked up by the red blood cells. When red blood cells carry carbon monoxide, they cannot also carry oxygen, so the cells of the body receive carbon monoxide instead of oxygen. When cells do not receive enough oxygen, they suffocate. The suffocation of cells caused by carbon monoxide is a condition known as *carbon monoxide poisoning*. Symptoms of carbon monoxide poisoning include a cherry red coloring of the skin, increased heart rate, dizziness,

◆ Wood-burning stoves release carbon monoxide into the air.

nausea, and unconsciousness. It can also cause death.

People can avoid exposure to carbon monoxide in several ways. In the home, they can keep heating systems and fireplaces clean and in good working order. People can also install carbon monoxide detectors in their homes. These devices sound an alarm to indicate when levels of carbon monoxide become dangerous. Keeping automobiles in good working order, and riding with the windows partly open, also helps reduce exposure to carbon monoxide. In addition, devices called CATALYTIC CONVERTERS installed in cars help reduce the carbon monoxide and other pollutants given off in automobile exhaust. [*See also* AIR POLLUTION; CARBON DIOXIDE; and PRIMARY POLLUTION.]

Carcinogen

◗A substance that causes CANCER. Carcinogens attack the body's normal cells, causing the abnormal growth of otherwise normal tissues to produce tumors, such as in lung or breast cancer, or diseased blood cells, as in leukemia. Some carcinogens attack the skin. Others enter the body through the nose, mouth, or other opening.

IDENTIFYING CARCINOGENS

To determine whether a certain material is a carcinogen, scientists test it on animals whose physical systems are similar to those of humans. If a large percentage of these animals develop cancer, scientists conclude that it might also cause cancer in people. The scientists also compare the health records of a group of people who have been exposed to a suspected cancer-causing agent with the health records of groups who have not been exposed. If members of the first group have a higher occurrence of cancer, the suspected material is determined to be a carcinogen. Some scientists believe VIRUSES may be potential carcinogens. They point to a virus associated with a rare form of leukemia and the fact that some carcinogenic tissues contain viruses similar to those causing cancer in animals to support their belief. According to cancer experts, RADIATION and chemicals are the main carcinogens in humans.

RADIATION

The sun's ultraviolet light is a carcinogen that causes skin cancer. As proof, scientists compared groups of people with inherited **melanin** skin tones, like African Americans and Asian Indians, with groups of Caucasians living in areas of intense sunlight. Further proof, scientists say, is that cancerous skin growths show up on body parts most often exposed to the sun, such as the face, neck, back of the hand, and on women's lower legs. Proof that other radiation is carcinogenic is evidenced from X RAYS and medical treatments that use radium, on-the-job exposure to radiation, and studies conducted with survivors of the atomic bomb blasts in Japan.

CHEMICAL CARCINOGENS

More than 100 years ago, doctors noted that people working with mineral oils and tars often developed skin cancer. Since then, hundreds of chemicals known to cause cancer in animals have been tested and found to be potential carcinogens for humans if present in food supplies or the ENVIRONMENT. Such chemicals can get into food supplies, sometimes as **additives** during food processing or during the growing process on farms. Some INSECTICIDES have carcinogens that pose a threat to humans, so the government prohibits or limits their use. Other cancer-related chemicals include those found in industrial and cigarette smoke, LEAD, ASBESTOS, vinyl chloride, chromium and iron compounds, some dyes, some natural food chemicals (fats have been associated with breast and colon cancer), and certain chemicals (artificial **hormones**) used in drugs.

A number of educational programs are available that show how to modify one's lifestyle as a method of preventing cancer. The programs provide tips on eating habits, exercise, and the value of physical examinations. [*See also* ENVIRONMENTAL PROTECTION AGENCY and ULTRAVIOLET RADIATION.]

Carnivore

▶ An animal that feeds on meat. Carnivores, also called PREDATORS, include large animals such as lions and wolves, and small animals such as snakes and spiders. A few PLANTS are carnivorous, such as the Venus's flytrap, sundews, and pitcher plants.

Biologists have specialized terms for some groups of carnivores. *Insectivores* are predators that eat only INSECTS and other INVERTEBRATES. Vultures or other carnivores that feed on the bodies of dead organisms are called *scavengers*. Carnivores that feed on other animals without killing them, such as leeches and mosquitoes that suck blood, are called *parasites*. Some carnivores may help control the numbers of the organisms on which they feed and thereby prevent OVERPOPULATION of the ECOSYSTEM.

The word *carnivore* also refers to MAMMALS in the order Carnivora, which includes cats, canines, weasels, and other similar mammals. Carnivores have claws and canine teeth, which they use to capture and kill their prey. [*See also* ADAPTATION; BIOLOGICAL COMMUNITY; FOOD CHAIN; FOOD WEB; HERBIVORE; OMNIVORE; PARASITISM; and PREDATOR.]

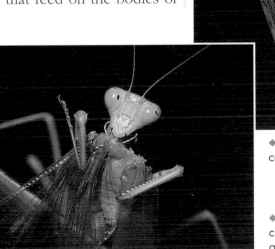

◆ The pitcher plant is a carnivorous plant.

◆ Research has determined that smoke from cigarettes is a major cause of lung cancer.

◆ The praying mantis is a carnivore, eating any other animal it can catch.

Carrying Capacity

The greatest number of individuals in a population that an ENVIRONMENT can manage over a long period of time. Population size is limited by many factors in the environment, such as the amounts of food, water, shelter, and sunlight available. The carrying capacity of an environment is reached when the environment can no longer support a growing population.

Carrying capacity can best be understood by studying how populations grow. A population will continue to grow as long as the birth rate exceeds the death rate. POPULATION GROWTH is unlike the growth of some other familiar things. For example, suppose you earn $1.00 for every job you do around your home. If you do two jobs, you earn $2.00; if you do three jobs, you earn $3.00. This type of growth is called *linear growth*, because the rate of growth is steady, and doesn't change from week to week. If linear growth is plotted on a graph, it looks like a straight line.

Populations do not show linear growth. Instead, they follow an S-shaped pattern known as EXPONENTIAL GROWTH. Exponential population growth is the increase in the size of the population in which the size of each new generation is a multiple of the previous generation. Exponential growth in a population is slow at first because the number of reproducing organisms is small. Growth becomes more rapid as the population size of each gener-

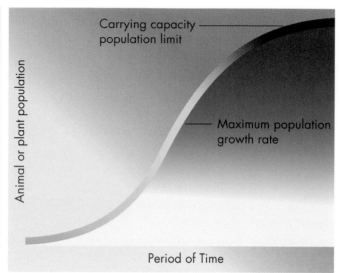

Populations of organisms follow an exponential growth curve, which has the shape of the letter *S*. When a population is no longer increasing in size, the carrying capacity of the environment has been reached.

ation increases. Often, exponential growth shows a doubling pattern. For example, 2 organisms become 4, the 4 become 8, the 8 become 16, and so on. With each increase the demands placed on the environment to meet the needs of all these individuals increase. Eventually, population growth stops altogether. The environment cannot sustain more individuals. The carrying capacity of the environment has been reached. At this point, the size of the population becomes fairly stable.

The carrying capacity of an environment can vary as conditions change with the time of the year. For instance, as WEATHER changes and becomes colder in winter, food supplies may become smaller and COMPETITION for food is fierce. Such conditions inhibit further population growth. In PLANT populations, carrying capacity may decrease in the summer months when water supplies become more limited. [*See also* DEMOGRAPHY and OVERPOPULATION.]

Carson, Rachel Louise (1907–1964)

Biologist and author whose book *Silent Spring* made the world aware of the dangers of PESTICIDES such as dichlorodiphenyl trichloroethane (DDT). On the first page of *Silent Spring* is a passage from a poem by John Keats: "The sedge is wither'd from the lake—And no birds sing." From these two lines came the idea for the title of the book—pesticides being sprayed indiscriminately were killing songbirds and thus bringing about a silent spring.

Rachel Carson was born on May 27, 1907, in Springdale, Pennsylvania. Her family lived on a small farm. There were chickens, cows, and horses, as well as woods for a youthful explorer. From early childhood, Rachel was encouraged to appreciate the beauty and wonder of nature. From her mother Rachel also learned to love books.

Rachel was certain that she would grow up to be a writer. At the age of 10 she had an article about Saint Nicholas published in *St. Nicholas* magazine, a publication for children.

At Pennsylvania College for Women, Carson pursued a degree in English. However, in her second year, she became interested in biology. After receiving a degree in zoology, Carson went on to earn her Master of Arts degree in zoology at Johns Hopkins University. After graduating, she taught zoology and spent summers studying at Woods Hole Marine Biology Laboratory in Massachusetts. Her experience at Woods Hole would inspire her to write her first two books— *The Sea Wind* and *The Sea Around Us*. From 1936 to 1952, Carson worked for the U.S. Bureau of Fisheries as a writer and biologist.

Carson possessed the talent to write poetic prose that painted word pictures of nature. "Where swarms of diminutive fish twinkle through the dusk like a silver rain of meteors," she wrote in an article entitled "Undersea," published in the September 1937 issue of *The Atlantic Monthly*. She brought to her talent as a writer a biologist's knowledge.

WRITING *SILENT SPRING*

Carson had written four books about the sea when she received a letter from a friend who lived in Cape Cod, Massachusetts. The writer described the effects of the state's spraying of DDT to kill mosquitoes. The DDT killed the BIRDS in her yard and woods. The mosquitoes remained, but the grasshoppers, bees, and other INSECTS were gone. Carson's friend asked her help in preventing future spraying.

As she contacted people about DDT spraying, Carson became aware of a great deal of information about pesticides. She began to realize that PESTICIDES threatened the natural world she loved. She began a four-year effort to write a book to describe the danger of pesticides.

"Everything that meant the most to me as a naturalist was being threatened and nothing I could do would be more important," she told a friend later.

Everything in *Silent Spring* was backed up by scientific research papers. Although it was a tedious job, Carson, the poet, took scientific fact and translated it into easy-to-understand words, such as these in the chapter entitled "Obligation to Endure": ". . . chemicals that have the power to kill every insect, the 'good' and the 'bad,' to still the songs of birds and the leaping of fish in the streams, to coat the leaves with a deadly film and to linger on in the soil." In the chapter "The Other Road," she called for people to "look about and see what other course is open to us" to control insect pests. She pointed to the wide range of insect control methods that did not harm the ENVIRONMENT.

GOVERNMENT TAKES NOTICE

Silent Spring was published as a serial beginning in the June 16, 1962, issue of *The New Yorker,* then later published as a book. Despite the storm of protests by chemical companies, the book was an instant success. Carson knew she had achieved her goal when a question about the book was put to President John F. Kennedy during an August 1962 press conference. The President said that he had requested a report on pesticides from his Science Advisory Committee. The report soon endorsed Carson's position that the risks of certain pesticides are poorly understood. The day after the report was released, a Senate committee began hearings on the environmental hazards of pesticides, including that of DDT.

Silent Spring had made the government and the people aware of the dangers of pesticides. The word spread around the world as the book was published in 14 countries.

Carson received many awards and honors for her book. The Schweitzer Medal of the Animal Welfare Institute meant the most to her. She had dedicated *Silent Spring* to Albert Schweitzer, the physician who spent his life treating the ills of Africans living in remote jungle villages. Carson admired and shared Schweitzer's reverence for life.

The awards, the commendations, and the medals kept coming. Sadly, Carson developed CANCER and soon was unable to attend the events and dinners honoring her. She died on April 14, 1964, at 56 years of age at her home in Maryland. In 1972, DDT was banned by government regulation. [*See also* AGRICULTURAL POLLUTION; BIOACCUMULATION; FUNGICIDE; and INSECTICIDE.]

Catalytic Converter

▶A POLLUTION-control device placed in the exhaust system of an AUTOMOBILE or other motor vehicle. During the 1980s, the federal government of the United States passed a law that required any new automobile sold in the United States to be equipped with a catalytic converter. A catalytic converter reduces the amount of pollutants an automobile releases into the ENVIRONMENT.

This is how a catalytic converter works. CARBON MONOXIDE and HYDROCARBONS are given off as waste products of gasoline combustion. A catalytic converter changes those waste products into water and carbon dioxide gas. Since water and

carbon dioxide cycle through the environment and are used by organisms, they are less harmful than are carbon monoxide and many hydrocarbons. Catalytic converters also change the NITROUS OXIDES in exhaust into nitrogen gas, the gas that naturally makes up about 78% of air.

Unleaded gasoline must be used in an automobile with a catalytic converter. The LEAD in leaded gasoline can collect on the metal beads that make catalytic converters work. If the beads are coated with lead, they cannot act as the catalyst of the chemical reactions that change the harmful compounds in exhaust into less harmful compounds.

Catalytic converters also work better when automobiles are kept tuned. A well-tuned automobile burns fuel more efficiently, reducing the amount of pollutants that must be converted by the catalytic converter. [*See also* AIR POLLUTION; CARBON DIOXIDE; CLEAN AIR ACT; and FOSSIL FUELS.]

CFCs

▶A group of human-made chemical compounds called *chlorofluorocarbons* (CFCs) that consist of the elements chlorine, fluorine, and CARBON. CFCs have been used as coolants in air conditioners and refrigerators, in the production of PLASTIC foams such as styrofoam, and as propellants in AEROSOL spray cans.

For many years, scientists regarded CFCs as rather safe chemicals. CFCs are not poisonous or flammable. In addition, CFCs are chemically stable; they do not combine with other chemicals or break down to form other substances. However, in-depth research began in the 1970s, when scientists realized that CFCs, which are stable on Earth, can break down in Earth's ATMOSPHERE. The public became concerned about the potential environmental effects of CFCs when scientists discovered that CFCs con-

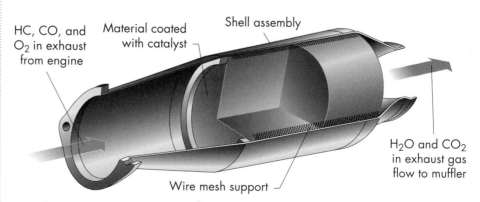

HC, CO, and O_2 in exhaust from engine

Material coated with catalyst

Shell assembly

Wire mesh support

H_2O and CO_2 in exhaust gas flow to muffler

◆ Catalytic converters are installed in the exhaust systems of cars to reduce the amounts of pollutants given off. Hydrocarbons (HC), carbon monoxide (CO), and oxygen (O_2) in exhaust are converted to harmless water (H_2O) and carbon dioxide (CO_2).

◆ Many air conditioners use CFCs as part of the air cooling system. The CFCs are dangerous to the atmosphere only if they leak out or are released when the air conditioner is damaged or disassembled.

tribute to the thinning of the OZONE LAYER.

The effects of CFCs on the ozone layer have been well studied. CFCs released on Earth gradually rise in the atmosphere, where the molecules are bombarded with ULTRAVIOLET RADIATION given off by the sun. Ultraviolet radiation causes CFCs to break apart and release single chlorine atoms. It is these chlorine atoms that make CFCs a threat to the ENVIRONMENT.

OZONE molecules are made up of three OXYGEN atoms that are chemically bonded. The oxygen from the atmosphere that you use for RESPIRATION contains two atoms of oxygen in each molecule. Chlorine atoms change ozone molecules in the atmosphere into two-atom oxygen molecules. This action results in a lessening, or depletion, in the overall supply of ozone in the atmosphere. It has been estimated that a single chlorine atom can break down as many as 100,000 ozone molecules.

The ozone layer of the atmosphere acts as a sunscreen for Earth. This layer protects Earth's organisms from dangerous ultraviolet radiation given off by the sun. Overexposure to ultraviolet radiation has been linked to skin CANCER and genetic damage.

In 1978, the United States banned the use of CFCs in aerosol spray cans. However, environmentalists remained concerned about the other sources of CFCs. World attention was once again focused on CFCs when scientists discovered an OZONE HOLE, an area of ozone thinning, above ANTARCTICA in 1984.

Since the discovery of the damaging effects of CFCs, scientists have looked for ways to reduce and eliminate the production of these harmful chemicals. In a conference held in 1992 about the problem of ozone depletion, 93 countries agreed to significantly reduce the manufacture and use of CFCs by the year 2000. [See also AIR POLLUTION; GREENHOUSE EFFECT; GREENHOUSE GAS; HYDROCARBONS; and MONTREAL PROTOCOL.]

Chemical Cycles

▮The natural cycling of chemical substances, such as water, CARBON, OXYGEN, nitrogen, and phosphorous, within ECOSYSTEMS. Chemical cycles involve substances important to life. Many chemicals are extracted from air, water, or the ground by living organisms, used in life processes; and either are passed into the ENVIRONMENT or on to other organisms that are PREDATORS or DECOMPOSERS.

Chemical cycles begin when nutrients are taken in by organisms from the air, SOIL, and water, or through the eating of other organisms. Once in an organism, nutrients are changed into biologically active substances. They are then returned to the environment through processes such as cellular RESPIRATION, PHOTOSYNTHESIS, and DECOMPOSITION. [See also ABIOTIC FACTORS; BIOGEOCHEMICAL CYCLE; and OXYGEN CYCLE.]

Chemical Spills

▮Any release, on land or water or into the ATMOSPHERE, of dangerous chemicals. As a consequence of accidents on highways, railways, and bodies of water, chemicals are spilled out of trucks, trains, and ships. Sometimes, as happened during the BHOPAL INCIDENT in 1984, the chemicals escape at their point of manufacture. The most spectacular accidents are highly publicized because they sometimes force the evacuation of communities or even decimate the population of a communiy.

For example, in 1976, in the village of Seveso, Italy, an explosion occurred at the Icmesa factory, where a HERBICIDE called 2,4,5-T was being manufactured. The accident released DIOXIN, which is extremely toxic. Although no deaths occurred at Seveso, 700 inhabitants were forced to leave

◆ Training exercises such as this were sponsored by the Maryland Emergency Management Agency to train personnel in hazardous waste cleanup.

◆ Some communities have instituted special collection days to ensure that hazardous household products are disposed of properly.

their homes, and 600 domestic animals were destroyed.

In the accident that occurred at Bhopal, India, on December 3, 1984, a cloud of methyl isocyanate escaped from a pesticide factory. The accident killed 2,500 people and injured 200,000 others.

The Persian Gulf war of 1991 produced another oil disaster and chemical spill. Iraqi military forces set fire to more than 700 Kuwaiti oil wells, spewing toxic chemicals into the Middle Eastern skies at the rate of 25,000 tons of CARBON DIOXIDE and 50,000 tons of SULFUR DIOXIDE per day.

With very little coverage by the media, some large chemical spills do not attract much public attention. In 1974, the Yugoslav ship *Cavtat* sank in the Adriatic. Its cargo hold was loaded with drums containing a compound called tetraethyllead. Legal arguments delayed recovery of the drums until the spring of 1978, when it was discovered that some of the drums aboard the sunken ship had begun to leak. Even then—in the face of the fact that lead compounds are among the most toxic in existence—the rate of leakage was deemed too slow to cause serious pollution.

At the LOVE CANAL disposal site of New York, the Hooker Chemical Company buried more than 40,000 tons (360,000 metric tons) of chemical waste between the early 1940s and 1953. Only after residents of the area had become alarmed by the high incidence of health problems and genetic damage was Love Canal seen as a major chemical spill.

Many potentially hazardous chemicals are used in homes, schools, and small business. Poured down drains or thrown out as trash, materials such as lead-based paint, household cleaners, batteries containing heavy metals, and PESTICIDES end up in sewage SLUDGE and solid-waste LANDFILLS. Increasingly, communities are adopting collection programs. In San Diego, California, for example, unused paint is recycled and used to cover graffiti. The vast majority of chemical spills pass unnoticed, however, simply because they are small. Even a small chemical spill can contaminate the environment, and a million such chemical spills every year add up, slowly, to become a very serious problem. [*See also* HAZARDOUS MATERIALS TRANSPORTATION ACT; HAZARDOUS SUBSTANCES ACT; HAZARDOUS WASTE; HAZARDOUS WASTES, STORAGE AND TRANSPORTATION OF; and TOXIC WASTE.]

Chernobyl Accident

❿The explosion of a nuclear reactor at Chernobyl, a small city in Byelorussia in the former Soviet Union, that sent radioactive emissions into the ATMOSPHERE. On April 26, 1986, the worst accident in history occurred at a nuclear power plant. The accident occurred during a test of the operation of the Chernobyl Nuclear Power plant.

Engineers conducting the test ignored regulations and temporarily shut down the plant's safety system to learn more about how the power plant worked. Two huge explosions and a fire occurred during the accident. The explosions blew the 1,000-ton (1,060-metric ton) con-crete lid off one of the plant's four nuclear reactors. RADIOACTIVE WASTE from the reactor's FUEL was released into the atmosphere. The harmful waste was carried by winds westward over Europe. Nearly 150,000 people living near the power plant had to be evacuated. In addition, these people had to be relocated eventually to avoid the dangerous conditions resulting from the RADIOACTIVE FALLOUT.

Officials from the Soviet Union reported that 36 people were killed by the fire and explosions. However, other authorities claim the number of deaths was closer to 300. Many medical experts are concerned about the future health of an additional 5,000 to 150,000 people. These experts believe those people likely will die a premature death due to RADIATION EXPOSURE. Such predictions are supported by

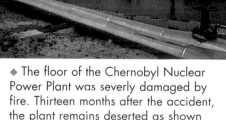

◆ The floor of the Chernobyl Nuclear Power Plant was severely damaged by fire. Thirteen months after the accident, the plant remains deserted as shown in the photo on the left.

Estimated Costs of the Chernobyl Accident (in Millions of Dollars)	
Power plant	1,040
Agricultural and export losses	1,220
Cleanup	350
Health and relocation	350
TOTAL	2,960

◆ **Note:** These are minimum estimates; other estimates of total financial loss resulting from the accident run as high as $5,130 million.

data that show that the number of children in villages near Chernobyl with thyroid CANCER has soared since the accident.

Today, the Chernobyl Nuclear Power plant is closed. The nuclear reactor has been enclosed in concrete in an effort to prevent additional RADIATION from escaping into the ENVIRONMENT. The total bill for cleanup at Chernobyl has been estimated at $14 billion.

The Chernobyl accident increased public awareness about the potential dangers of nuclear power plants. At the same time, engineers have learned important lessons about nuclear power plant design and construction. [*See also* ALTERNATIVE ENERGY SOURCES; CARCINOGEN; NUCLEAR FISSION; RADIOACTIVITY; and THREE MILE ISLAND.]

China Syndrome

See NUCLEAR POWER

Chlorination

▮Water-purification process in which chlorine is added to water supplies to kill disease-causing microorganisms. Chlorine is added to water before and after it is filtered at a WATER TREATMENT plant. The chlorine added before filtration controls the growth of ALGAE and other organisms so that the filtration process is more effective. The chlorine added after filtration prevents BACTERIA and other disease-causing organisms from growing in the water.

Chlorination eliminates about 99.9% of the disease-carrying germs from water. After chlorination became widespread in the United States during the early 1900s, there was an immediate decrease in ccurrence of diseases such as typhoid and cholera. Today, not only water, but also SEWAGE, is treated with chlorine to prevent the transmission of diseases.

Despite its success in preventing disease, chlorination is somewhat controversial. Some of the chemicals formed when chlorine reacts with organic matter may cause CANCER in humans. Other disinfectants now are being tested as possible substitutes for chlorine, but they are less effective than chlorine and also pose health risks. [*See also* PATHOGEN; WATER QUALITY STANDARDS; and WATER TREATMENT.]

Chlorofluorocarbons

See CFCS

Clay

See SOIL

Clean Air Act

▮Law originally passed by Congress in 1963, and updated in later years (1965, 1967, 1970, 1977, 1990), that authorizes the federal government to set up and enforce a set of national air-quality regulations, award grants, and direct investigations aimed at stopping or limiting AIR POLLUTION. In particular, under the original Clean Air Act, standards were set to control the emissions of **pollutants** from AUTOMOBILES and to curb the amounts of industrial pollutants released in areas in which the air had already become dirty. It is the responsibility of the ENVIRONMENTAL PROTECTION AGENCY (EPA) to see that the act is carried out.

AUTOMOBILE EMISSIONS

Motor vehicles emit most of the CARBON MONOXIDE and HYDROCARBONS in the air. Under the 1970 Clean Air Act regulations, the amount of carbon monoxide emitted by automobiles was to be reduced by almost 75% of the current standard. Emission of hydrocarbons and NITROGEN OXIDES were also limited. Photochemical SMOG, a brown haze that results from the action of sunlight on hydrocarbons and nitrogen oxides, contributes to the formation

photochemical oxidants oxygen agents produced by the interaction of sunlight and chemicals.

pollutants waste materials that contaminate air, soil, or water.

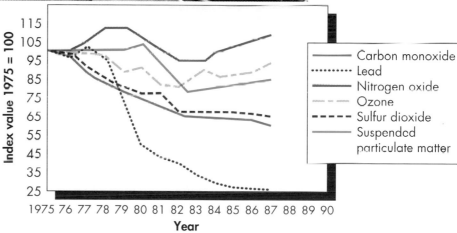

◆ Chemical engineers monitor air pollution by collecting pollutants from air samples and measuring their concentrations.

of OZONE. Reducing the emissions of these two components would help to keep **photochemical oxidants** within the allowable limits.

INDUSTRIAL EMISSIONS

Industrial plants emit most of the sulfur oxides and PARTICULATES—fine particles of ash, soot, and heavy metals—in the air. The 1970 Clean Air Act requires plants to produce no more than 80 micrograms of SULFUR DIOXIDE per cubic meter of air and 75 micrograms per cubic meter of particulates, on average, in one year. Industrial centers are held to the same emission levels for nitrogen oxides and photochemical oxidants as automobiles because both sources create about the same amounts of these pollutants.

ROLE OF THE STATES

Although the federal government sets the goals for improved air quality, the states must enforce measures to meet these goals. States were given until 1972 to present plans to the EPA spelling out how they intended to meet the standards

Legend:
- Carbon monoxide
- Lead
- Nitrogen oxide
- Ozone
- Sulfur dioxide
- Suspended particulate matter

◆ Air pollution in the United States has been reduced substantially as a result of the Clean Air Act.

for automobiles and industries. After the EPA accepted a state's plan, the state had until 1975 to put its clean-air plans into action. The automobile manufacturers' deadline was extended to 1980.

CRITICISMS

Critics of the Clean Air Act complained that reducing particulate and sulfur dioxide emissions to the new levels would force large cities, like New York, to increase the use of low-polluting NATURAL GAS, which, at the time the act was revised, was in short supply. Large cities would also have to limit or ban peak-hour commuting, the critics argued, and build new, nonpolluting MASS TRANSIT systems that would cost millions of unavailable dollars. Therefore, most large cities could not meet the law's deadline.

TOWARD THE TWENTY-FIRST CENTURY

The latest revision of the Clean Air Act, which was passed by Congress in 1990, further limited the emissions from automobiles—60% less nitrogen oxides and 40% fewer hydrocarbons by the year 2003—and required that pollution-control equipment must last at least ten years. For industrial plants, emissions of sulfur dioxide must be reduced by 50% by the year 2000 and nitrogen oxides must be reduced by 33%. The use of chloro-fluorocarbons (CFCS) and other chemicals threatening Earth's protective OZONE LAYER was banned. A 90% reduction in the amounts of toxic and cancer-causing chemicals from factories and businesses was also ordered.

For the smoggiest U.S. cities, including Chicago, Los Angeles, New York, and Houston, even more reduction of auto emissions was stipulated, and cleaner-burning gasoline has to be sold in such cities. For California, auto makers must build one million cars using cleaner ALTERNATIVE ENERGY SOURCES (ELECTRICITY, natural gas) or cars equipped with special emission-reducing tailpipes by the year 2000.

According to the 1990 changes, many of the cleaner-air provisions would be phased in over a period of 15 years. This was done to help businesses and to protect the jobs of Americans who work for them. For the first time, the Clean Air Act revisions also set standards for small businesses, such as auto-repair shops and dry cleaners. To comply with the new regulations, both big and small businesses have

◆ Emission controls on motor vehicles have helped reduce air pollution.

to invest money in pollution-control equipment.

To raise the money to pay for pollution control equipment, businesses will have to pass the cost on to consumers or lay off workers. It is estimated that to pay for changes in auto emissions, consumers will pay 6–10% more per gallon (3.78 liters) for gas by the year 2000, and an average of $600 more for a new car by the year 2003. It could cost an additional $3 billion a year for coal-burning utilities to change to burning low-sulfur FUEL or install SCRUBBERS to ensure clean emissions. This would result in a rise in utility rates for Americans.

Some experts estimate that consumers will pay an average of $300 to $400 more each year by the time all of the act's regulations go into effect. Many Americans feel that in a COST-BENEFIT ANALYSIS, having cleaner, healthier air to breathe is worth any price they have to pay. However, not all agree. [See also ACID RAIN; ATMOSPHERE; BEST AVAILABLE CONTROL TECHNOLOGY (BACT); GREEN-HOUSE EFFECT; and HEAVY METALS POISONING.]

Clean Water Act

▶ Federal legislation designed to improve the quality of water in coastal and inland waterways of the United States. Passed in 1972, the Clean Water Act is the main body of law protecting the nation's waters from WATER POLLUTION. The main goal of the Clean Water Act is to "restore and maintain the chemical, physical, and biological integrity of the nation's waters."

Government involvement in protecting the nation's waters began with passage of the Water Pollution Control Act in 1948. This legislation gave state and local governments the funding needed to deal with water pollution problems. Federal funding increased during

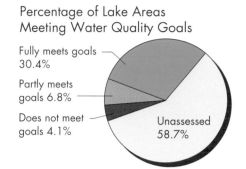

Percentage of River Miles Meeting Water Quality Goals

Fully meets goals 20.1%

Partly meets goals 5.8%

Does not meet goals 3.0%

Unassessed 71.1%

Percentage of Lake Areas Meeting Water Quality Goals

Fully meets goals 30.4%

Partly meets goals 6.8%

Does not meet goals 4.1%

Unassessed 58.7%

the 1950s and 1960s. However, it wasn't until 1972, with the passage of the Water Pollution Control Amendments, that the federal government took on a more important role in protecting U.S. waterways. Under the new federal laws, direct discharge of large amounts of toxic pollutants into U.S. waterways is prohibited. The laws also called for protection of U.S. WETLANDS, and for more financial assistance to communities that operate SEWAGE TREATMENT PLANTS.

The Water Pollution Control amendments gave polluting industries a deadline of July 1, 1977, to control a amounts of organic waste, oil, grease, SEDIMENT, acid, BACTERIA, and VIRUSES in their discharged EFFLUENT. By 1983, industries were also required to install the BEST AVAILABLE CONTROL TECHNOLOGY (BACT) to meet the goal of eliminating all water pollutants by 1985.

The Water Pollution Control Amendments were revised in 1977 and again in 1987. In general, the changes also strengthened the 1972 laws. The revisions also placed a greater emphasis on toxic substances and nonpoint pollution. Another important group of laws designed to protect water resources includes the 1972 MARINE PROTECTION, RESEARCH, AND SANCTUARIES ACT. [*See also* INDUSTRIAL WASTE TREATMENT; MARINE POLLUTION; NATIONAL POLLUTANT DISCHARGE ELIMINATION SYSTEM (NPDES); NONPOINT SOURCE; OCEAN DUMPING; SEDIMENTATION; SEWAGE; SEWAGE TREATMENT PLANT; SLUDGE; SURFACE WATER; WASTEWATER; and WATER QUALITY STANDARDS.]

Clear-cutting

The harvesting of FORESTS in which all trees are removed from an area. In whole-tree clear-cutting, all the above-ground tree matter is removed from a harvested site. In complete-tree clear-cutting, both the above-ground and below-ground tree matter are removed.

In some areas, seedlings are planted to replace trees that are cut down. This produces a group of trees more even in age or size that can be harvested at one time later on. Sometimes a single variety of crop is planted, a practice called MONOCULTURE, in the clearing and then harvested all at once at the appropriate time.

When an area is clear-cut, its BIODIVERSITY is lost. This results in HABITAT LOSS that leads, in some cases, to the EXTINCTION OF PLANT and animal SPECIES. For example, overharvesting in the northwest part of the United States has threatened not only the SALMON fishing industry but the very existence of various interior forest species as well. Both

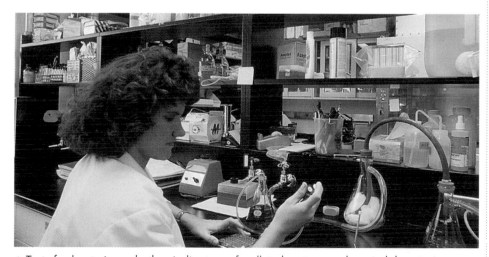

◆ Tests for bacteria and other indicators of polluted water are done in laboratories.

◆ An area of this forest has been clear-cut. Replanting in this area will prevent it from becoming a wasteland.

◆ When there are no trees to hold it in place, soil in steep slopes is carried away into nearby rivers.

the NORTHERN SPOTTED OWL and the marbled murrelet are now considered endangered under the terms of the ENDANGERED APECIES ACT, and populations of lynx, marten, fisher, and others appear to be declining.

Forests have been called "the Earth's lungs," because they remove much CARBON DIOXIDE and release significant amounts of OXYGEN and water vapor into the ATMOSPHERE. As more forests are cleared, carbon dioxide concentrations rise, contributing to the GREENHOUSE EFFECT. As a result, a region's CLIMATE becomes hotter and drier.

When trees are no longer present to hold SOIL in place, exposed TOPSOIL is carried away by wind and water. This is especially true if a clear-cut is conducted on a steep slope. Soil caried away from a clear-cut area ends up in rivers and other waterways, creating further problems. In the Pacific Northwest, for example, the billion dollar commercial salmon fishing industry has greatly declined because of over-harvesting of trees in areas near spawning WATERSHEDS. A deforested area might regenerate into forest, or become an eroded wasteland, depending on local conditions, how the cutting is done, at what time of the year the forest is cut, and whether replanting is done.

The effects of clear-cutting on tropical RAIN FORESTS are especially devastating. The nutrients that support lush plant growth in tropical regions do not exist in the thin topsoils, but in the vegetation. When the forests are cleared and not replaced, only nutrient-poor clay soil remains.

Less than 2% of tropical forests are protected from clear-cutting practices. The result is that tropical forests continue to be cleared at the rate of about 38.5 million acres (15.6 million hectares) per year. The destruction of forests in places like Central and South America stems in great part from efforts in these areas to create jobs and agricultural land for large populations. [*See also* AGROFORESTRY; CONIFEROUS FOREST; DEFORESTATION; FOREST; FOREST PRODUCTS INDUSTRY; FOREST SERVCE; FORESTRY; and OLD-GROWTH FOREST.]

Climate

▶ The summary of WEATHER conditions of an area over an extended period of time. Weather refers to what is happening in the ATMOSPHERE at a certain time. Climate is the average weather in a geographic area over a long period of time, including such conditions as the temperature, amount of PRECIPITATION, humidity, and number of hours of sunlight an area receives.

Climate is important to life on Earth because it determines the types of organisms that can survive in a particular area. For example, DESERT organisms have a number of ADAPTATIONS for surviving in a geographic area that receives very little water. Organisms that live in polar climates are adapted to conserving heat.

FACTORS THAT DETERMINE CLIMATE

Climate is determined by a variety of factors. These factors include latitude, air circulation, OCEAN CURRENTS, and the local geography of an area. Latitude is perhaps the most important factor of climate because it has the most direct influence on average yearly temperature.

Latitude

Meteorologists recognize three general climate zones based on latitude: polar, temperate, and tropical. *Latitude* is the distance north and south from the equator, measured in degrees. Latitude helps determine a region's temperature

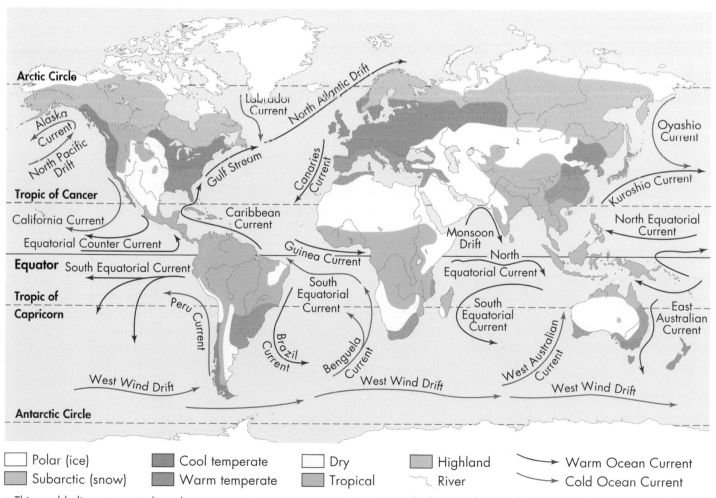

Polar (ice) Cool temperate Dry Highland ⟶ Warm Ocean Current
Subarctic (snow) Warm temperate Tropical River ⟶ Cold Ocean Current

◆ This world climate map is based on average temperatures, precipitation, and other weather conditions over a long period of time.

because it influences the amount of sunlight an area receives. For instance, at the equator (0° latitude) the sun is directly overhead year-round and its rays strike Earth's surface directly. Sunlight is concentrated on a small surface area. That is why tropical areas (23½° north latitude to 23½° south latitude) have the hottest year-round temperatures.

In polar zones (66½° north and south latitudes), the sun is lower in the sky. Its rays strike Earth at a more indirect angle, causing the rays to spread out over a larger area. In addition, some of the sunlight is lost when it is reflected off polar ice. This explains why polar regions have the lowest annual temperatures.

Between the tropical and polar zones are the temperate zones. The continental United States is in a temperate zone. In temperate zones, weather generally changes with the seasons. Winters are cold and summers are hot. The spring and fall seasons are characterized by mild temperatures.

Ocean Currents

Of course, climates are more complex than just the three general divisions of polar, temperate, and tropical. Within each zone, a variety of other factors affect climate. Ocean currents, for example, have a great effect on climate. Nearness to OCEANS tends to make climates more moderate. This is why coastal areas tend to have warmer winters and cooler summers than inland areas. Oceans are also the source of most of the precipitation that falls on land. As a result, coastal areas usually get more precipitation than inland areas.

Air Circulation Patterns

Air circulation patterns help determine the amount of precipitation an area receives. In tropical regions where the sun's rays strike Earth directly, air near the surface is warmed and becomes less dense, causing it to rise. Warm air can hold a lot of water, which evaporates from the oceans and land. As the warm air rises, it begins to cool and loses some of its ability to hold water. Thus, in the tropics it rains heavily.

Warm tropical air also determines the amount of precipitation that falls in other parts of the world. The warm air of the tropics forces cooler air in the atmosphere to move toward the poles. This cooler air falls back to Earth at a latitude of about 30°, warming as it falls. As this warm, dry air moves across Earth's surface, it creates extremely dry conditions. This movement of air explains why most of the world's deserts, including those in the southwestern United States, occur near 30° latitude. [*See also* BIOME and CLIMATE CHANGE.]

Climate Change

▷ A significant, measurable difference in the WEATHER patterns of an area over a period of time. Climate change refers to the weather conditions of an area over time. Such

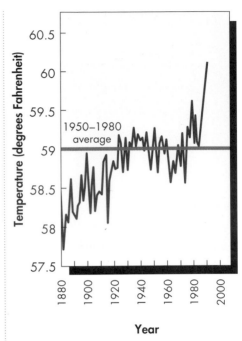

◆ The average global temperature has increased since 1880.

conditions include temperature, humidity, PRECIPITATION, and wind patterns. Many scientists are concerned that human activities may be causing changes in Earth's ATMOSPHERE, which in turn may be altering CLIMATES around the world.

DETERMINING FACTORS OF CLIMATE

The climate of an area generally remains fairly stable over a few decades. However, over thousands and millions of years, an area's climate fluctuates considerably. For example, scientists have identified several ICE AGES during Earth's history. During the ice ages, vast portions of the land were covered by sheets of ice. The last ice age began about two million years ago and ended about 11,000 years ago.

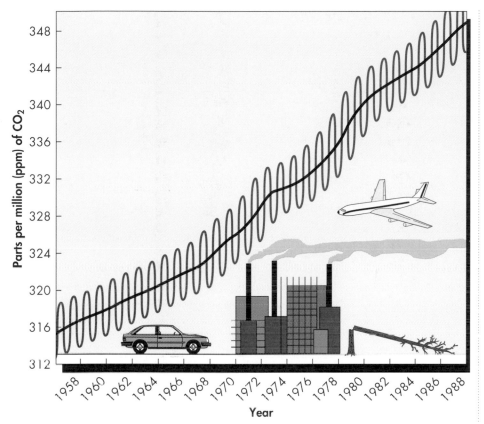

◆ Scientists are concerned that our increasing use of fossil fuel is causing an increase in carbon dioxide in the atmosphere. This, in turn, may change the global climates.

◆ Industrial air pollution is a source of greenhouse gases.

◆ Scientists use various methods, such as sending instruments up in the air, to measure changes in temperature.

Scientists cannot pinpoint the exact causes of changes in Earth's climate like those that brought about the ice ages. However, scientists do know that energy from the sun is the driving force of climate. Sunlight warms the atmosphere, causing water on Earth's surface to evaporate. In the air, this water becomes humidity and eventually precipitation, such as rain or snow. Warm air also expands and rises, whereas cooler air falls. This movement of air is the basis for winds at Earth's surface.

Except for the changing of the seasons, climate in an area generally stays the same from year to year. This occurs because an area receives about the same amount of sunlight year after year, according to its position on Earth.

HUMAN IMPACTS ON CLIMATE

Minor, year-to-year differences, as well as drastic, long-term changes in a region's climate, such as ice ages, are examples of natural climate change. Scientists are also studying how human activities may be affecting climate. Many studies have pointed to the burning of FOSSIL FUELS, such as COAL and oil, as a human activity that may be altering Earth's climate. When these fuels are burned, they release large amounts of CARBON DIOXIDE into the atmosphere. In one study from Hawaii's Mauna Loa research station, scientists have shown that carbon dioxide levels in the atmosphere have increased sharply since 1958. Carbon dioxide, as well as METHANE, OZONE, NITROGEN OXIDE, and CFCS, are important GREENHOUSE

GASES. Greenhouse gases contribute to the GREENHOUSE EFFECT—the trapping of heat close to Earth's surface. Other sources of the increase in carbon dioxide in the atmosphere are the destruction of tropical RAIN FORESTS (PLANTS absorb carbon dioxide, so a loss of plants in an area results in an increase in carbon dixoide) and an increase in the number of AUTOMOBILES and power plants, which emit carbon dioxide into the air.

Many scientists suggest that a warmer atmosphere could dramatically affect precipitation and wind patterns on Earth. Such changes in climate could disrupt natural ECOSYSTEMS as well as the quality of human lives. Not all scientists agree about the long-term impact of global climate change, and the governmental and international policies to address this issue are still controversial. [*See also* ABIOTIC FACTORS; BIOME; CARBON CYCLE; GLOBAL WARMING; METEOROLOGY; SOLAR ENERGY; and ULTRAVIOLET RADIATION.]

Climax Community

▶A mature ECOSYSTEM in which the populations of PLANTS, animals, and other organisms remain relatively stable over a long period of time. The climax community is the final stage in a process known as *ecological succession,* the natural process of development and change in the number and kinds of organisms in an area.

In general, climax communities are characterized by having large plants and trees with long life cycles, high SPECIES DIVERSITY, complex FOOD WEBS, and efficient cycling of nutrients, such as water, CARBON, and nitrogen. A climax community can take many years to develop. The amount of time depends upon a variety of factors, including CLIMATE, types of animals and plants present, and levels of POLLUTION.

STAGES

The steps leading to a climax community are generally similar. In the early stages of SUCCESSION, there are few animals and plants, and BIO-

◆ A beech and maple forest in Michigan is an example of a climax community.

◆ Large plants and trees are often found in climax communities.

DIVERSITY is low. These early SPECIES are typically hardy, such as weeds, with a high reproductive output and the ability to withstand severe changes in the ENVIRONMENT. Dandelions, for instance, are very common in the early stages of ecosystem development because they quickly produce seed heads that hold several hundred seeds.

As time goes on, species diversity slowly increases. FOOD CHAINS are simple at first and include only PRODUCERS, primary CONSUMERS, and a few DECOMPOSERS. Slowly, the food chains become more complex and eventually contain higher TROPHIC

LEVELS and a greater variety of decomposers.

As these changes occur, the ecosystem functions more efficiently. The large and diverse plants of climax communities trap more sunlight during PHOTOSYNTHESIS, making more food available for consumers. The more complex food webs result in a greater use of the food energy produced by plants. The cycling of nutrients, such as nitrogen and phosphorous, is also in balance.

The result of ecological succession is a climax community containing species that are able to resist minor changes in CLIMATE as well as COMPETITION from invading species.

The activities of the organisms in climax communities usually do not change the environment. Climax communities are said to be in equilibrium; that is, they will remain generally unchanged unless disturbed by NATURAL DISASTERS, such as flood or fire, or disrupted by human activities.

Occasionally the equilibrium of climax communities is disturbed. For instance, in the northeastern United States, beech and maple trees dominate the climax FORESTS. However, fallen trees in the forests create openings in the forest canopy enabling FERNS, weeds, wildflowers, and other small plants to thrive on the sunny forest floor. In other areas of a forest, occasional FOREST FIRES disturb the forest and the process of succession begins again. In other words, a forest can best be thought of as a constantly changing patchwork of stable and unstable areas. [*See also* ECOLOGY and PIONEER SPECIES.]

Clouds

❚ The visible collections of tiny water droplets, ice crystals, or both that are suspended in the ATMOSPHERE. Clouds are classified into three main types—cirrus, cumulus, and stratus—based on their characteristics. Cirrus clouds are wispy. Cumulus clouds appear in heaps that are usually located between 6,000 feet (1,830 meters) and 20,000 feet (6,100 meters) above Earth's surface. Ice-filled cumulus clouds may be located at an altitude of about 35,000 feet (10,700 meters). Stratus clouds are low clouds that

◆ Cirrocumulus clouds may indicate a storm.

◆ Cirrostratus clouds are high clouds formed entirely of ice crystals.

◆ Stratus clouds extend over large areas and usually bring rain or snow.

◆ Wispy white cirrus clouds are made of tiny white crystals and are found at high altitudes.

◆ Cumulus clouds have distinct, rounded outlines.

◆ Cumulonimbus clouds extend to great heights and sometimes bring tornadoes.

appear in layers. These clouds usually are located between ground level and 5,000 feet (1,625 meters) above Earth's surface.

Individual clouds may have a combination of characteristics. The names of such clouds describe their combined traits. Cloud names may also contain prefixes or suffixes that describe the cloud's traits. For example, the prefix *alto-*, which means "high," the prefix *nimbo-*, which means "rain," and the suffix *-nimbus,* which also means "rain," commonly appear in the names of clouds. Thus, *stratocumulus* describes high clouds that are heaped up on top of each other.

Similarly, the term *cumulonimbus* describes clouds in towering heaps that have flat bottoms. Because these clouds are associated with heavy rain and thunderstorms, they are often called *thunderheads.*

SULFUR DIOXIDE and other pollutants in the air may mix with water droplets in clouds to form acids. Such acids that fall from the atmosphere to Earth are called acid precipitation. Most often, acid precipitation falls as ACID RAIN. Acid rain is carried by the movement of clouds from industrial areas. Often it is in one section and deposited on FORESTS and farmland in another area. Damage resulting from acid rain has been severe in some parts of the United States, Canada, and northern Europe. In some lakes, acid rain has changed the conditions so much that the ECOSYSTEM can no longer support PLANT or animal life. [*See also* AIR POLLUTION; SMOG; and WEATHER.]

Coal

▶A solid FUEL formed from the remains of PLANTS that lived on Earth millions of years ago. Like PETROLEUM (oil) and NATURAL GAS, coal is a FOSSIL FUEL. The name *fossil fuel* is used to identify fuels that formed from the remains of organisms that lived on Earth millions of years ago.

Coal differs from the other fossil fuels in two important ways. First, coal is a solid fuel; oil exists as a liquid, while natural gas, as its name implies, exists as a gas. Second, coal formed from plant matter, mostly decaying FERNS that existed on Earth during the Carboniferous period, about 345 to 280 million years ago. Petroleum and natural gas formed mostly from the remains of marine organisms.

COAL FORMATION

During the Carboniferous period, many parts of Earth now covered by dry land were covered by swamps. Ferns, many as large as trees, were the dominant plant of these swamps. When these plants died, their remains collected at the bottom of the swamps. Over time, the remains of more plants, along with other SEDIMENTS, collected on top of the dead plant matter and sediment on the swamp bottom. As additional layers of plant matter and sediment accumulated on top of earlier layers, the pressure created by the added weight of the new layers compacted and forced water out of the layers beneath them. In addition, heat resulting from the weight of upper layers acted upon the dead plant matter at the lowest layers. Over time, the actions of heat and pressure changed the plant matter into the solid rock called coal.

The formation of coal is a long and slow process that occurs in a series of stages. Each stage in coal formation produces matter with properties different from those of the other stages. The four stages in coal formation are PEAT, lignite, bituminous coal, and anthracite coal.

Peat

The first stage in the formation of coal results in a material called *peat*. Peat is a compacted mass of plant material that resembles wood. Because it is not rock, peat is not a true form of coal. However, the formation of peat is a necessary step in the formation of coal.

Peat forms very close to Earth's surface and contains a large amount of water and a small amount of CARBON. In many parts of the world, peat is burned as a fuel. However,

◆ Peat.

◆ Anthracite coal.

◆ Lignite coal.

Coal goes through four stages as it forms. Each stage has different traits and is therefore suited to different uses.

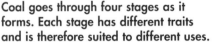

◆ Bituminous coal.

◆ Underground coal mining causes several environmental problems.

coal is sometimes burned in coal stoves in homes to produce heat for the home and for cooking.

Anthracite Coal

The final stage in coal formation results in a hard coal called *anthracite coal*. This coal forms very deep within the Earth, where it is acted upon for millions of years by great heat and pressure. Anthracite coal has a shiny black color and has the lowest water content and highest carbon content of any form of coal.

Anthracite coal produces the greatest amount of heat and the smallest amount of smoke of any form of coal. These properties of anthracite coal make it the most desirable form of coal for use in homes. Because it is much less abundant than any other form of coal, anthracite coal is also the most costly form of coal to use.

PROBLEMS ASSOCIATED WITH COAL USE

The use of coal as a source of heat and electricity has the same drawbacks as does the use of other fossil fuels. These drawbacks include problems associated with the availability and the mining of coal, as well as various forms of POLLUTION.

Availability

Different types of coal are in relative abundance in the United States and other parts of the world. However, because coal takes millions of years to form, it is being used faster than it can be replaced by nature. For this reason, coal is considered a NONRENEWABLE RESOURCE.

because of the large amount of water in peat, it produces a great deal of smoke as it burns.

Lignite

Over millions of years, layers of plant matter and sediment may collect on top of peat beds. The heat and pressure generated by these layers compact the peat, forcing out water and gases that were trapped in spaces between the plant materials. As the peat becomes more compacted, it changes into a rock material called *lignite*. Lignite is a soft, brown form of coal that contains less water and more carbon than peat. Lignite forms deeper beneath Earth's surface than does peat and is removed from Earth through MINING. Like peat, lignite is burned as a fuel. However, lignite gives off much less smoke than does peat.

Bituminous Coal

Lignite may be acted upon by heat and pressure to form a type of coal called *bituminous coal*. Bituminous coal contains less water and more carbon than lignite and is harder than lignite. The fairly high carbon content and low water content of bituminous coal allows this coal to give off less smoke than either lignite or peat. Bituminous coal also gives off more heat as it burns. Thus, bituminous coal is in greater demand for use as a fuel than either lignite or peat.

Bituminous coal is the most abundant type of coal in the United States. Because it forms deeper in Earth than does lignite, deep shafts must be dug for its removal. The main users of bituminous coal in the United States are power plants that burn the coal to generate ELECTRICITY and industry. Bituminous

Mining of Coal

To get the coal needed to meet the energy demands of people, it must be mined from Earth. The digging of mines is very disruptive to the natural ENVIRONMENT of a region in several ways. First, for a mine to be dug, large amounts of SOIL must be removed from Earth's surface. The removal of soil creates a loss of HABITAT for growing plants. In addition, as the native plants are removed from an area, other organisms that use these plants for food or shelter must leave the area if they are to survive.

Mining coal also creates pollution problems for both land and water. As coal is removed from Earth, waste material generated from the mining process is often placed in piles surrounding the mine area. These piles, called *spoil piles,* often contain substances, such as compounds of sulfur, LEAD, and COPPER, that are harmful to organisms and the environment. As rain falls in the area, water from the rain passes through and mixes with the substances and materials contained in spoil piles. The rainwater may then carry these substances into nearby soil or into groundwater supplies. Harmful substances that enter the soil may make it unsuited to plant growth, causing the plants to die. This, in turn, may disrupt FOOD CHAINS by eliminating the food sources for other organisms that feed directly or indirectly on the plant matter. Harmful substances that enter groundwater may pollute AQUIFERS used by people for their freshwater supply. In addition, harmful substances in groundwater may be carried to lakes and streams, making these habitats unsuitable for organisms.

Air Pollution

All fossil fuels give off some amount of smoke when burned. This smoke can be irritating to the eyes and respiratory systems of people and other organisms. The smoke also contains harmful substances such as CARBON MONOXIDE, NITROGEN DIOXIDE, SULFUR DIOXIDE, and PARTICULATES such as ash and soot. Each of these substances is directly harmful to humans and other organisms. In addition, these substances are also harmful to the environment. For example, nitrogen dioxide given off by industrial smokestacks can react with sunlight to form a yellow-brown haze called *photochemical smog.* Photochemical smog gives the air a "dirty" appearance. It can also be irritating to the eyes and respiratory systems of people.

Another common environmental problem associated with the burning of coal and other fossil fuels is acid PRECIPITATION, usually in the form of ACID RAIN. Acid rain forms when sulfur and nitrogen compounds combine with water in the ATMOSPHERE to form acids, which return to Earth when it rains or snows. Acid precipitation can be very harmful to land and water environments. For example, when this rain falls on land, it changes the pH of soil, often making the soil unable to support the growth of many types of plants. Acid rain has a similar effect when it falls into lakes and streams. In addition, acid rain is destructive to buildings and stone monuments made by people. Over time, acids falling onto stone structures begin to break apart the structures in a process called *chemical weathering.*

SOLVING THE PROBLEMS ASSOCIATED WITH COAL USE

Solving the problems associated with coal use is not easy, but efforts are being made. Because of the amount of time required for coal to form, no one can increase the

◆ Spoil piles made up of waste material from coal mining destroys habitat in the surrounding area.

amounts of coal available for use by people. However, through CONSERVATION and development of ALTERNATIVE ENERGY SOURCES, current supplies of coal can be made to last longer. In their search and development of alternative energy sources, scientists are looking for ways to meet the energy needs of people that make use of RENEWABLE RESOURCES that are readily available and less polluting to the environment than fossil fuels. Some resources scientists have explored include the use of nuclear energy, SOLAR ENERGY, and wind energy. Although each of these resources has the benefits scientists look for when developing alternative energy sources, they also have many drawbacks. Thus, use of these alternative energy sources is limited.

Combating the pollution problems associated with the burning of coal has largely resulted from the combined effects of legislation and efforts of people in technology. In the United States, several laws have been passed to help reduce the amounts of coal burned and to help clean the smoke given off by burning coal. These laws include the CLEAN AIR ACT, the Air Quality Act, and the Acid Precipitation Act. Each of these acts requires industries to find ways to use less energy, use energy more efficiently, and reduce the amounts of pollutants produced from the burning of coal and other fuels.

Technology is helping industries reduce the amounts of pollutants given off by the burning of fuels. Some methods industries are using to accomplish this goal include the use of filters and devices called *electrostatic precipitators* and SCRUBBERS.

Electrostatic Precipitators

Electrostatic precipitators are devices that remove particulates from the emissions given off by coal-burning industries. As particulates pass through the device, they are given an electrical charge that causes them to be attached to the walls of the device. Periodically, the current in the device is turned off. When this happens, the particulates lose their attachment to the wall and fall to the bottom of the device. Once at the bottom, they are collected and removed. By using electrostatic precipitators, industries may remove as much as 99% of the particulates present in coal smoke.

Scrubbers

Scrubbers are devices that are placed within the smokestacks of power plants and other industries. These devices remove both particulates and sulfur dioxide gases from smoke. In a smokestack equipped with a scrubber, smoke is passed through a fine mist of water. The water traps particulates and sulfur dioxide gases. As these materials collect in the water, they form SLUDGE. The sludge is collected and disposed of in an appropriate manner. Like electrostatic precipitators, scrubbers remove about 99% of the particulates contained in coal smoke. They also remove as much as 85% to 95% of sulfur gases. [*See also* AIR POLLUTION; CARBON DIOXIDE; GREENHOUSE EFFECT; HABITAT LOSS; INDUSTRIAL WASTE TREATMENT; NATURAL RESOURCES; NITROGEN OXIDES; RESTORATION BIOLOGY; and TOXIC WASTE.]

Coevolution

A situation in which two or more SPECIES evolve structures and behaviors in response to each other. An organism's survival depends upon interactions with other organisms. For example, some species hunt and kill other species in predator-prey relationships. The types of interactions between species can influence the EVOLUTION of a species just as interactions with the physical or ABIOTIC FACTORS of the ENVIRONMENT influence evolution.

When two organisms live so close together that the survival of one species depends on the survival of the other, it is necessary for each organism to adapt to changes

◆ Together, bees and flowers have evolved structures and behaviors that enable bees to gather nectar at the same time they pollinate flowers.

that take place in its coexisting species. Such changes are evidence of coevolution. One of the most dramatic examples of coevolution is demonstrated by interactions between FLOWERING PLANTS and bees. Some species of flowering plants rely upon animals, such as BIRDS, INSECTS, and small MAMMALS, for POLLINATION. Bees are one of the most common insect pollinators.

To attract insects, many flowers are brightly colored and have pleasant odors. Evidence indicates that bees cannot see the color red, which may explain why bee-pollinated flowers are usually blue or yellow. In comparison, the tropical plant species *Rafflesia* is pollinated by a fly species that feeds upon decaying organisms. To attract these flies, the *Rafflesia* flower emits an odor that smells like rotting meat. The flowers have evolved these ADAPTATIONS in response to their pollinators.

Coevolution is common between plants and the organisms that feed upon them. Although plants do not move from place to place, they are not defenseless. For instance, many types of plants, such as poison ivy and poison oak, produce chemicals that discourage or kill other organisms. Cabbage plants produce chemicals that are harmless to humans but highly toxic to most species of insects. An insect called the cabbage butterfly has evolved the ability to break down these chemicals. In this instance, cabbage plants evolved a defense mechanism against most insects. However, in response, cabbage butterflies evolved a way to break down the chemical defense. [*See also* MUTUALISM and SYMBIOSIS.]

Cogeneration

▶The use of thermal and electric energy from a single source. When power plants burn FOSSIL FUELS (oil, COAL, NATURAL GAS), ELECTRICITY is not the only form of energy produced. Heat energy, such as steam or hot water, is also given off during the process. By using the heat given off by furnaces and boilers, cogeneration systems make use of energy that would otherwise be wasted. A simple example of cogeneration is a car heater that uses heat from the engine to warm the inside of the car.

Cogeneration systems are most commonly used by power plants. In New York City, Detroit, and other U.S. cities, electric companies are now using waste heat from their powerful generators to heat their own buildings. In Europe, heat from power plants is supplied to many industrial and commercial buildings.

Large industries in the United States also use cogeneration. For instance, the paper industry, which produces large amounts of steam as a waste product in the papermaking process, uses cogeneration to produce some of the electricity used to run its plants. [*See also* ALTERNATIVE ENERGY SOURCES and ENERGY EFFICIENCY.]

Commensalism

▶A close association between SPECIES in which one organism benefits without harming or helping the other organism. Commensalism is an example of SYMBIOSIS, a close, long-term relationship between species.

Nature is filled with examples of commensalism. One interesting example of this relationship is demonstrated by the female boxing crab and the tiny marine animals called *sea anemones*. The sea anemones live on the claws of the female boxing crabs. The

◆ This crab receives protection from the stinging sea anemones without harming or helping the anemones.

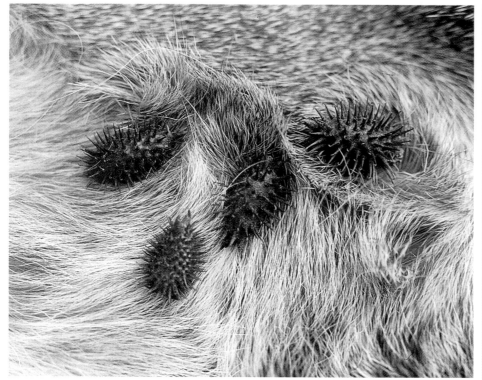

◆ Cocklebur seeds in a donkey's hair. In an example of commensalism, cockleburs depend on animals to disperse its seeds.

anemones are equipped with tiny, stinging animal cells. To protect the eggs she carries beneath her abdomen, the female crab uses the anemones by covering her claws with them, turning the claws into boxing gloves. When a PREDATOR approaches, the crab takes a poke at the animal with her "gloved" claw. The predator, stung by the anemones, quickly retreats. In this relationship, the crab receives protection from the sea anemones. The sea anemones appear to be neither harmed nor helped by the relationship.

Commensalism is very common in plant species. Such relationships have been observed in mosses, FERNS, orchids, and other PLANTS. In tropical RAIN FORESTS, the leaves and thick branches of the tall trees provide a covering so dense that sunlight cannot reach the FOREST floor. As a result, the forest floor is too dark to permit many small plants to survive. Some small plants, such as orchids and mosses, often grow on tree branches high in the forest canopy, where they can get ample sunlight. The trees receive no benefits from this relationship. They also do not appear to be harmed. [*See also* ADAPTATION.]

Community

See BIOLOGICAL COMMUNITY

Competition

▶A relationship between two or more SPECIES in which each contends against the others for such resources as food or living space. Two different species in the same community are in competition with one another if there is a limited amount of one or more resources needed for survival by these species. An increase in the number of different species that need the same resource also results in competition. For example, deer, turkeys, and squirrels eat acorns. Tree swallows, bluebirds, and starlings need nesting sites. Grass and dandelions use nitrogen in the soil. If the number of acorns, the number of good nesting sites, and the amount of nitrogen in the soil are limited, there will be competition for those resources.

In a small pond, there is only enough space and resources to support a small number of PLANTS. Insect larvae and FISH that feed on the plants must compete with each other for food. Only those insect larvae and fish that get enough to eat will grow and mature.

SOME RESULTS OF COMPETITION

When competition between two species for the same niche is great, one species may be eliminated from the niche. This is called the *competitive exclusion principle*. If a competing species is not eliminated, it may remain in the area only in small numbers. Often, a compet-

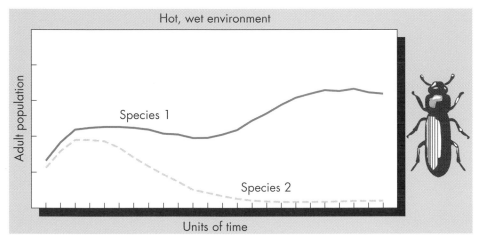

Hot, wet environment

Adult population

Species 1

Species 2

Units of time

◆ Curves show alternative outcomes for the two species of flour beetles in the cool-moist climates.

process, which included mutations that changed beaks, enabled the different finches to adapt to different food sources. When they flew back to the original island, they were no longer in competition with the species that had remained, and, in fact, had evolved into a new species.

LABORATORY EXPERIMENTS IN COMPETITION

Competition between species has been observed in laboratory experiments. For example, in an experiment done by Dr. Thomas Park at the University of Chicago, two different species of a flour beetle were made to live in the same location. The location was a jar of flour. Each species survived in the flour jar if it lived alone. However, when the other species was put into the jar, the two species entered into a relationship of competition. The experiment called for changing the temperature and humidity in the experimental jars so that there were six different combinations of these factors. One species survived better in the hot-wet environments. The other survived best in the cool-dry environments. In the in-between combinations, sometimes one species won out and sometimes the other species won out. This is an example of competition. [*See also* EVOLUTION; INSECTS; and POPULATION GROWTH.]

ing species must leave an area and relocate elsewhere to survive.

In some instances, competition may be a factor in the creation of new species, or *speciation*. This has happened in the GALÁPAGOS ISLANDS off Ecuador. Charles DARWIN found that there were many species of finches, differing in size, shape, and use of beaks, on different islands. He theorized that the ancestors of all species were blown from mainland Ecuador by a freak storm many, many years before and soon found themselves in competition for the limited food supply.

Groups flew to nearby islands and were separated from the main population. The subpopulations became specialized for feeding on different things such as insects, worms, and seeds. An evolutionary

◆ The gooseneck barnacle is in competition with the acorn barnacle for food and space.

Composting

▶The production of nutrient-rich SOIL from the decay of organic matter, such as leaves, grass clippings, and leftover food scraps, using microorganisms and by managing environmental factors such as temperature and moisture. Composting produces a natural fertilizer called *compost* that looks very different from the materials from which it is formed. The composting process involves the action of AEROBIC microorganisms present in the soil. In this process of decay, the bulk of the raw materials is reduced. Thus, the compost is more easily stored and used than its original components.

THE COMPOSTING PROCESS

To prepare compost, a warm, moist place where decay can occur is needed. Usually, a compost pit is dug or the raw materials are stacked above ground. Dead plant materials—leaves; plant cuttings; grass; potato, banana and orange peels; apple cores; coffee grounds; and other plant parts—are placed in the pit or piled on the ground in a layer about 6 inches (15 centimeters) deep. Next, a thin layer of soil or manure is added atop the plant matter. These materials speed decay and help the matter remain moist. Additional layers of dead plant matter and thin layers of soil or manure are added to the compost pile. Finally, water is added to the mixture to encourage decay.

The matter making up the compost must decompose for 5 to 7 months before it becomes a useful soil additive. Compost may also be used as a mulch that is placed on top of the soil to hold in moisture for plant growth. Composting processes range from those done in backyards to those done in large municipal SOLID WASTE facilities. [*See also* BACTERIA; BIODEGRADABLE; DECOMPOSERS; DECOMPOSITION; FUNGI; and RECYCLING, REDUCING, REUSING.]

◆ In composting, organic matter, such as leaves and leftover food scraps, are acted on by microorganisms to produce compost.

◆ Many people build compost heaps in their backyards to produce their own natural fertilizers.

Comprehensive Environmental Response, Compensation, and Liability Act of 1980 (CERCLA)

▶ A law passed by Congress in 1980 to protect communities from the dangers of HAZARDOUS WASTES. The project has been nicknamed the SUPERFUND, and $10.6 billion has been allocated to meet the obligations of the Comprehensive Environmental Response, Compensation, and Liability Act (CERCLA). The Superfund is mainly funded by taxes on crude oil, PETROLEUM products, PETROCHEMICALS, certain inorganic chemicals, and a general corporate Superfund tax.

The law authorizes the federal government to oversee cleaning up HAZARDOUS WASTE dumps; to make polluters pay for cleanups; to develop a national priorities list of sites requiring urgent cleanup; to take emergency actions in areas where there are spills or accidental releases of hazardous wastes; and to encourage research for the reduction, treatment, and disposal of hazardous wastes.

The Superfund has helped communities like LOVE CANAL, New York, and Times Beach, Missouri, where residents were forced to leave their homes, which were built on hazardous waste sites. The SOIL, SURFACE WATER, and groundwater in these areas had been contaminated with chemical wastes that had been improperly disposed of during previous decades.

Since 1980, only 12% of existing hazardous waste sites have been cleaned up under the CERCLA program, due to the impasse and delay in Congress to formulate standards for cleanup. As of 1993, only 161 sites had been cleaned up while another 1,256 sites remained on the national priorities list. [See also ENVIRONMENTAL PROTECTION AGENCY (EPA); HAZARDOUS SUBSTANCES ACT; HAZARDOUS WASTE MANAGEMENT; and HAZARDOUS WASTES, STORAGE AND TRANSPORTATION OF.]

◆ An EPA worker in protective gear works at a Superfund cleanup site.

Coniferous Forest

▶ A large area in which the dominant SPECIES of PLANTS are cone-bearing trees. Conifers are trees that produce their seeds in cones. In addition to cones, most conifers have leaves that remain green and on the tree throughout the year. Individual conifer leaves do drop off the trees. However, the leaves do not develop the variety of colors and do not all drop off the tree in autumn as do the leaves of deciduous trees.

The leaves of most conifers are covered by a waxy coating that helps prevent the loss of water during dry periods. In addition, the leaves of conifers generally have a smaller surface area than do the leaves of deciduous trees. However, the shapes of the leaves of conifers do vary somewhat. These variations in leaf shape are one way different types of conifers are distinguished from each other. For example, conifers having needlelike leaves include members of the fir, pine, spruce, larch, and hemlock families. Yews and redwoods are conifers that have flattened, oblong leaves. A third group of conifers includes the cedar, cypress, and juniper. These trees have small, scalelike leaves.

◆ This forest in Mt. Shasta, California, is a coniferous forest.

There are two types of coniferous forest—the TAIGA and the montane. The FORESTS differ in their locations, CLIMATE, and the types of trees that grow in the region. The forests also differ widely in the animal species they support.

THE TAIGA

The taiga is often referred to as the northern coniferous forest. This forest stretches in a broad band across the Northern Hemisphere, just south of the TUNDRA region that characterizes the ARCTIC. At its southern boundary, the taiga of North America reaches into Canada and the northernmost parts of the states of New England and the Pacific Northwest.

Because of its location, the climate of the taiga is characterized as cold and fairly dry. Winterlike WEATHER conditions may occur for six to ten months of the year.

The parts of the taiga nearest the tundra border have growing seasons as short as two months. The growing season may be as long as four months in the southernmost part of the region. Little PRECIPITATION falls in the taiga, making the region fairly dry. The heaviest precipitation falls as rain during the growing season. The rest of the year, small amounts of precipitation fall as snow because of the cold temperatures of the region.

In the northernmost part of the taiga, the dominant tree is the spruce. Because moose are also common in this region, the area is often referred to as the "spruce-moose belt." Farther south, dominant taiga conifers include pine, hemlock, and cedar. The waxy coating and shape of the leaves of these trees are ADAPTATIONS that help these trees retain water during the drier winter months. In addition, the overall shape of the trees (which is somewhat triangular) and the great flexibility of their branches are adaptations that prevent too much snow from collecting on branches and damaging the trees.

Individual leaves shed from conifers generally collect and decompose slowly beneath the trees. As the leaves decompose, they release acidic substances into the SOIL. The acidity of the soil, along with limited light beneath the trees, prevents the growth of many types of plants on the forest floor. However, mosses, some FERNS, and a few bushlike plants such as blueberries, do thrive in these conditions. LICHEN—a symbiotic association between FUNGI and an ALGAE—are the other dominant PRODUCERS of the area.

During the growing season, INSECTS, FISH, and migratory BIRDS are common in the lakes and bogs of the taiga. Other animals such as moose, gray wolves, arctic hare, arctic foxes, and lynx live in the taiga throughout the year. All these animals have adaptations that allow them to survive the cold, harsh climate of the region. For example, arctic foxes and hare have smaller ears that help them conserve body heat than do their relatives living in warmer climates. In addition, the coloring of these animals changes from white in winter to brown during the growing season to help the animals blend with their surroundings.

MONTANE FORESTS

Coniferous forests that lie south of the taiga are generally called *montane forests*. Many montane forests develop in mountainous regions, where climate conditions become colder and more winterlike as altitude increases. In these regions, the tops of high mountains are cold and covered by snowfall even when surrounding low-lying areas are experiencing temperate climate conditions. Conifers that thrive at the higher altitudes of these mountains include spruce, alpine fir, and bristlecone pines. Lower on the slopes, dominant conifers include Douglas fir and ponderosa pine.

In the western United States, montane forests have developed on the western slopes of the Rocky Mountains, the Sierra Mountains, and the Cascade Mountains. The largest of all conifer species, the giant Sequoia, is common along the slopes of the California Sierras. In the northeastern United States, montane forests exist throughout many of the New England states as well as into Pennsylvania and New Jersey. Similar montane forests also exist in parts of Europe and as far south as Mexico and Guatemala.

The climate conditions of the montane are generally not as harsh as those of the taiga. For example, with the exception of high mountains, winterlike conditions of very low temperatures and heavy snowfall exist for only about three to four months of the year. In addition, the montane receives a greater amount of precipitation throughout the year than does the taiga, thus its growing season is longer.

The milder climate conditions of montane regions allow these areas to support a greater variety of WILDLIFE than does the tundra. The moist conditions of the montane allow the region to support the growth of a variety of mosses and ferns in addition to some grasses. These plants, in turn, attract a huge variety of insects and birds, such as chickadees, warblers, finches, and thrushes, which feed on the insects. The warmer and milder climate of the montane also allows the region to support a variety of fungi. The fungi work with BACTERIA to carry out their roles as DECOMPOSERS in the ENVIRONMENT. The presence of these decomposers helps to recycle nutrients through the ECOSYSTEM and makes the soil of the montane more nutrient-rich than that of the taiga.

The animal life of the montane is also extremely diverse and varies widely depending upon the location of individual forests and the distribution of lakes, ponds, and streams within the forests. Frogs are common AMPHIBIANS living near montane lakes and ponds. Various types of snakes, tortoises, and other REPTILES live in the more temperate

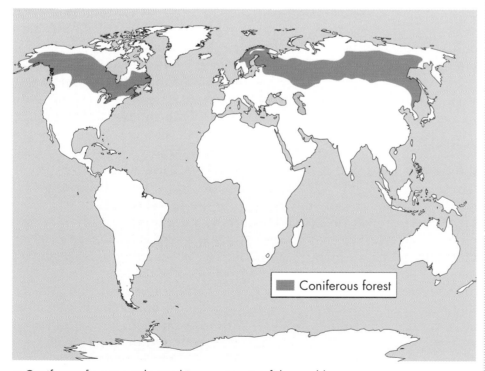

◆ Coniferous forests are located in many parts of the world.

Coniferous forest

parts of the the montane. Common forest MAMMALS include such diverse animals as white-tail deer, moles, raccoons, rabbits, oppossum, black bear, and beaver. Many predatory birds, including various species of owls and hawks, also make their homes in montane forests. [*See also* BIODIVERSITY; BIOME; DECIDUOUS FOREST; RAIN FOREST; and WETLANDS.]

Conservation

▶The careful use of NATURAL RESOURCES in a way that helps keep them available for use by future generations. Human beings use Earth's resources extensively. Resources can be divided into two categories: RENEWABLE and NONRENEWABLE. Renewable resources include living organisms and sunlight. Nonrenewable resources include MINERALS, such as nickel, platinum, and gold and FOSSIL FUELS. Fossil fuels are formed from the incompletely decomposed remains of PLANTS that lived several hundred million years ago. When these organisms died, they were buried underneath Earth's surface. Over time, these organisms changed in form to become PETROLEUM, COAL, or NATURAL GAS.

CONSERVATION OF RENEWABLE RESOURCES

A renewable resource has the capacity to replenish itself, even though some of that resource may be removed from time to time. Every

◆ The aim of conservation is to preserve scenic areas such as this one from being polluted.

SPECIES has the potential to reproduce itself in numbers greater than those that survive. Therefore, conservationists feel that the excess can be put to human use, as long as care is taken not to deplete breeding populations or threaten the existence of the species.

The aim of conservation is to manage or regulate the use of a resource so that it does not exceed the capacity of the species to renew itself. Conservationists recognize that the rapidly growing number of people in the world must be fed, clothed, and housed. They believe that to meet these needs, renewable resources should be used over nonrenewable resources whenever possible. If managed properly, renewable resources can be replaced as they are used. In contrast, preservationists want to ensure the continuity of species and ECOSYSTEMS

regardless of their potential usefulness. Preservationists would not cut down old-growth forests; a conservationist would allow an old-growth forest to be cut down carefully in such a pattern as to leave many trees standing to maintain the ecosystem, maintain the soil, and prevent destruction of the land, at the same time allowing part of the renewable resource to be used for society's needs.

Today, many conservation efforts focus on tropical RAIN FORESTS that are found in many of the world's fastest growing nations. Tropical rain forests have the greatest BIODIVERSITY of any terrestrial BIOME. However, this potential renewable resource is being threatened as rain forests are being cleared at a rapid rate for economic and industrial purposes. Conservation efforts include establishing

◆ These men are planting grass as part of a prairie restoration program.

◆ One way of conserving energy is by using mass transit.

◆ Wastes from urban developments often pollute coastal areas around the world.

plantations of trees and using products of existing trees, instead of cutting them down.

There are many other ecosystems and HABITATS to be considered in conservation efforts. SAVANNAS could be managed in such a way that they can continue to be a source of food for the people of Africa and South America.

Worldwide, the aquatic ecosystems and WETLANDS are in danger. Coastal systems are critical to the health of the OCEANS. Nutrients from the land are washed into the ocean. Ocean plant life depends on these nutrients for growth. Ocean animal life is dependent on plant life. Most of the world's marine life are caught in coastal areas because this is where their food is located. Therefore, it is important that these areas are not destroyed by POLLUTION, overfishing, and urban development.

CONSERVATION OF NONRENEWABLE RESOURCES

Most of the energy used by industrial nations come from fossil fuels, which are nonrenewable. Some estimates show that oil will last about 30 more years, gas about 50 more years, and coal about 1,000 more years. These estimates are based on the present rate of use. As developing countries become industrialized, this rate of use may increase and these fuels may be used up more quickly. Coal can be transformed for oil and gas, but the process is expensive and uses up an enormous amount of energy.

To conserve fuel resources and to meet the needs of people,

ALTERNATIVE ENERGY SOURCES are presently being explored and used. Some of these include the use of renewable resources such as SOLAR ENERGY and WIND POWER to generate ELECTRICITY. NUCLEAR POWER is another alternative source of energy. However, it uses URANIUM, a nonrenewable resource, and brings with it a host of potential problems, such as those that occurred at THREE MILE ISLAND and Chernobyl. For these reasons, the nuclear industry's growth has been slowed.

As part of conservation efforts, individuals, businesses and governments have all been active in the recycling, reducing, and reusing resources. To encourage these practices, the United States passed the RESOURCE CONSERVATION AND RECOVERY ACT (RCRA). Many individual states have also passed laws requiring the recycling of cans, bottles, and paper.

There are many other ways to conserve energy. One way is to use MASS TRANSIT instead of AUTOMOBILES. Another way is to design buildings so they take advantage of natural conditions and use solar energy. Cycling the heat generated by the production of electricity for use as steam in the process called COGENERATION is another way.

CONSERVATION OF WILDLIFE HABITATS

There has been much pressure in the United States and elsewhere to protect species whose existence and survival are threatened. Congress has passed many laws to save individual species and to prevent habitats from being destroyed. These laws include the ENDANGERED SPECIES ACT, the MARINE MAMMALS PRO-TECTION ACT, the MARINE PROTECTION, RESEARCH, AND SANCTUARIES ACT, the RECLAMATION ACT OF 1902, the WILD AND SCENIC RIVERS ACT, and the WILDERNESS ACT.

In 1968, the U.S. DEPARTMENT OF THE INTERIOR's *Conservation Yearbook* stated that humans are a threatened species because overpopulation and uncontrolled technology threatens the environment. The secretary of the interior said that "the time has come for us to evolve an ecology of man in harmony with the constantly unfolding ecologies of other living things." When we do this, we will be employing the tools of the conservationist.

Conservation Easement

▮A private legal agreement or other legal restriction that determines how a specific parcel of land will be used. A conservation easement guarantees that LAND USE is no longer under the landowner's control.

Although conservation easements may be granted for a certain time period, they usually last for life. By legally binding all future owners of such land to respect the agreement, conservation easements have become a way to protect WILD-LIFE HABITATS and scenic and historic areas. For example, a conservation easement may give the easement owner the right to preserve a particular land region as a WILDERNESS area. Such an easement would prohibit the owner of the land from HUNTING, MINING, or performing any other actions that would be contrary to the easement. [*See also* CONSERVATION; PUBLIC LAND; and WILDLIFE CONSERVATION.]

Consumer

▮Any organism that obtains its nutrients and energy by feeding on other organisms. Organisms that are able to make their own food using the energy of the sun or certain chemicals are called PRODUCERS. Producers, also called AUTOTROPHS, include PLANTS, ALGAE, and several species of BACTERIA and protists. Animals, FUNGI, many SPECIES OF BACTERIA and most protists cannot make their own food. These organisms are consumers. Consumers are also called *heterotrophs*. By feeding directly on producers or by eating other organisms, consumers help pass nutrients and energy through an ECOSYSTEM.

HERBIVORES, CARNIVORES, AND OMNIVORES

Scientists classify consumers into several groups depending upon how they obtain their energy. For instance, some consumers, such as grazing horses, seed-eating BIRDS, algae-eating FISH, and fruit-eating monkeys, feed only on plants or other producers. Consumers that feed only on producers are called HERBIVORES.

◆ Sea otters are carnivores that eat up to a fifth of their body weight daily.

Many consumers, such as lions, leopards, sharks, and owls, feed only on other consumers. Consumers that feed only on other consumers, or only on products of consumers, such as eggs, are called CARNIVORES. Carnivores are commonly referred to as meat-eaters.

Many carnivores such as lions must hunt, kill, and eat other animals. Such carnivores are called PREDATORS. The organism a predator eats is called the *prey*. Other carnivores do not have to kill to obtain their food. Instead, they eat the remains, or *carion*, of animals that have already died. Carnivores that obtain their food in this way, such as vultures and hyenas, are called *scavengers*. Scavengers perform an important ecological role by clearing the bodies of other organisms from the ENVIRONMENT.

Humans are an example of another type of consumer. Most humans do not eat only plant or only animal products. Instead, people generally eat a diet that includes a variety of foods that come from both plants and animals. Because of this mixed diet, humans are called OMNIVORES. Other examples of omnivores include bears, raccoons, and coyotes.

DECOMPOSERS

Some organisms break down and decay dead organisms for food. Such organisms are known as DECOMPOSERS. Fungi and many species of bacteria are examples of decomposers. Decomposers obtain their nutrients and energy by breaking down complex organic compounds into simpler compounds. Once the compounds are broken down into usable forms, they can be absorbed by the decomposer. It is this process of breaking down food matter before it is absorbed that distinguishes decomposers from scavengers. Scavengers break down food matter inside their bodies, after they have eaten the matter.

Types of Consumers and Some Examples

Type	Examples
Primary consumers	snails, honeybees, aphids, (herbivores) weevils, ungulates, sparrows, millipedes, fungi, protozoa
Omnivores	bears, raccoons, chimpanzees, human beings, cockroaches, rats
Secondary consumers	cats, spiders, dragonflies, (carnivores) Portuguese man-o'-war, monitor lizards, centipedes
Scavengers	vultures, flies, tumblebugs, burying beetles
Tertiary consumers	wolverine, shark, praying mantis, (carnivores) orca, starfish, ladybug beetles
Decomposers	fly larva (maggots), bacteria, fungi

Decomposers play one of the most ecologically important roles in the ecosystem. By breaking down organic substances into simpler substances, decomposers help recycle nutrients back into the SOIL, where they can be used once again by growing plants.

CONSUMERS AND THE FOOD CHAIN

To show how nutrients and energy are passed from one organism to another in an ecosystem, biologists use a model known as a FOOD CHAIN. Each organism in a food chain represents a feeding step, or TROPHIC LEVEL, in the passage of nutrients and energy. Plants and other producers always occupy the first trophic level in a food chain.

Because there are several types of consumers, these organisms can occupy different trophic levels in an ecosystem. For example, herbivores are known as first-order consumers because they feed directly on producers. Herbivores, therefore, always make up the second trophic level of a food chain.

Second-order consumers, or carnivores, make up the third trophic level. Carnivores are meat-eaters that feed on first-order consumers. Carnivores may also eat at higher trophic levels. For example, third-order consumers are animals that feed on second-order consumers. An alligator eating a carnivorous fish or a snake eating an insect-eating frog is an example of a third-order consumer. Fourth-order consumers are those that feed on third-order consumers, and so on until a step in the food chain is reached at which no organism

(other than decomposers) feeds at the highest level. Animals that feed at the higher level in a given food chain are usually the dominant predators in the ecosystem. [*See also* BIOLOGICAL COMMUNITY and NICHE.]

Consumer Waste

See RECYCLING, REDUCING, REUSING

Container Deposit Legislation

Laws that help reduce litter and encourage recycling. In 1972, the Oregon legislature passed the state's first container law. The law

required a deposit of two to five cents on cans and bottles for beverages such as soft drinks and beer. It was estimated that drink containers made up 62% of the state's litter. Within two years after the law

◆ Many states have laws mandating recycling of bottles.

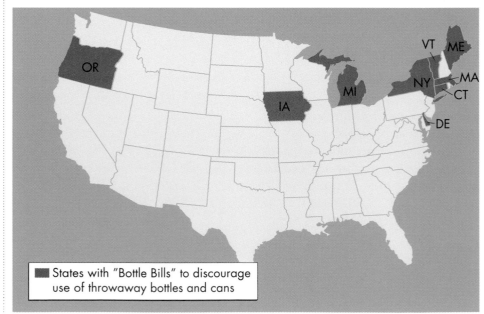

■ States with "Bottle Bills" to discourage use of throwaway bottles and cans

went into effect, container litter decreased by about 49%.

Eleven other states have since enacted similar container laws—California, Connecticut, Delaware, Florida, Iowa, Maine, Massachusetts, Michigan, New York, Rhode Island, and Vermont. Such legislation is also on the books in the Netherlands, Scandinavia, the Commonwealth of Independent States, Canada, Japan, parts of Australia, and some developing nations.

States with container laws report increases in recycling and decreases in roadside litter and the need for LANDFILLS. Some people are calling for a national container bill. If enacted, it could save about 7.8 million tons (7 million metric tons) of glass, 2.2 million tons (2 million metric tons) of steel, and 0.56 million tons (0.5 million metric tons) of lumber each year. [See also RECYCLING, REDUCING, REUSING.]

Continental Drift

▶ A **theory** that states that all the continents were once connected in a single landmass and are slowly drifting about the surface of the planet. Continental drift was proposed in 1912 by German **meteorologist** Alfred Wegener (1880–1930). Wegener called the original landmass Pangaea, which means "all Earth." According to Wegener, Pangaea broke apart about 200 million years ago.

WEGENER'S EVIDENCE FOR CONTINENTAL DRIFT

Wegener supported his idea with two major pieces of evidence. First, he saw that if the present continents were pushed together, they would almost fit together like the pieces in a jigsaw puzzle.

Second, the distribution of certain PLANTS and animals suggests that the continents were once connected. For example, the fossils of a REPTILE named *Mesosaurus* were found in South America *and* in Africa. Wegener thought it was unlikely that the reptile swam across the ocean from one continent to the other. Instead, he proposed that *Mesosaurus* lived on both continents when they were connected in Pangaea.

THE LANGUAGE OF THE ENVIRONMENT

meteorologist a scientist who studies weather and climate.

theory an idea that has been tested many times and is generally accepted as fact.

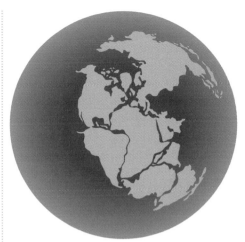

200 million years ago

100 million years ago

Present day

◆ Shown above are the stages of Earth's land masses breaking up over time.

The theory of continental drift is widely accepted by scientists today. However, it was rejected by most scientists during Wegener's lifetime, because he was not able to explain how continental drift could have occurred.

HOW PLATE TECTONICS EXPLAINS CONTINENTAL DRIFT

In the 1960s, a new explanation for how the continents move was proposed. The new theory, called PLATE TECTONICS, states that Earth's crust and upper mantle are broken into 15 sections called *plates*. The plates are like rafts that float and move on the semi-solid mantle below. These slowly moving plates carry the continents.

Scientists propose that forces deep inside Earth cause the plates to move. They estimate that the continents move horizontally at a rate of 75 inches (190 centimeters) each year. [*See also* CONVERGENT EVOLUTION; EVOLUTION; and LITHOSPHERE.]

◆ Contour farming helps prevent topsoil erosion by reducing runoff.

Contour Farming

▶A method of preparing land for plant growth in which the land is plowed across a slope instead of down it. The EROSION OF TOPSOIL is one of the greatest threats to agriculture. It occurs when wind, running water, or other agents carry away SOIL from the land. One method used by farmers to prevent erosion caused by running water is contour farming. In contour farming, land is plowed across, rather than down, a slope. Such plowing creates furrows between rows of crops that hold water instead of allowing the water to flow freely downhill. In this way, soil is prevented from washing downhill.

Contour farming has proved to be one of the most effective ways of preventing topsoil erosion. However, this technique is useful only in areas with sloped land. In such areas, contour faming often is used along with a farming method called *strip-cropping,* in which sections of plowed land are separated from each other by strips of crops. [*See also* AGROECOLOGY and SUSTAINABLE AGRICULTURE.]

Convention on International Trade in Endangered Species of Wild Fauna and Flora (CITES)

▶An agreement signed in 1975 by representatives from 80 countries that banned commercial trade in hundreds of SPECIES of endangered animals and PLANTS. The Convention on International Trade in Endangered Species of Wild Fauna and Flora (CITES) agreement also stipulated that 239 other animal and plant species could be traded only if permission were granted by both the importing and exporting nations.

The limitations on commercial trade in endangered animals imposed by CITES included trade not only the living animal but also trade of any goods from the animals, such as their hides, furs, ivory horns, or other body parts. By 1994, the list of CITES countries totaled 120.

POACHING

Despite the rulings set down by CITES, officials found it hard to enforce the law. During the first 20 years of the agreement, the rhinoceros population of Asia and Africa dropped from 100,000 to less than 10,000. The number of TIGERS in Asia plummeted from 100,000 to about 5,000 in the same period. Some poachers, or illegal hunters, killed even more of the ENDANGERED SPECIES after CITES went into effect because they made more profits from the hard-to-obtain animal products. For example, in China and Taiwan, a rhino horn earned a poacher up to $30,000 for 1 pound

(0.45 kilograms), and 0.035 ounces (1 gram) of powdered tiger bone sold for $500. Both products have been used in traditional medicines for generations. In 1995, the Environmental Investigation Agency (EIA), based in Washington, DC, discovered rhino horn in 20 of the 40 pharmacies it checked in Taiwan and tiger bone in 13 of the 21 medicine shops it checked there. At the same time, China admitted to having at least 5 tons (4.5 metric tons) of rhino horn stored for future use.

CITES COMPLIANCE BEGINS WITH CONSUMERS

To control POACHING, some people believe we must first stop the demand for poached goods. As long as people around the world demand items such as coats made from endangered cats, **scrimshaw,** ivory from elephant tusks, ashtrays made from gorilla hands, or powdered rhino and tiger bones, poachers will continue to kill these endangered animals and smuggle their parts to be sold on the black market. As long as people are willing to pay high prices for rare trop-

◆ Confiscated bounty from poachers and smugglers who kill endangered animals and deal in animal parts.

ical monkeys, parrots, or orchids, smugglers will meet the demands.

In her book *If You Love This Planet,* Helen Caldicott, M.D., states that as a member of the South Australian National Parks and Wildlife Council in the 1970s, she discovered that smugglers drugged Australian cockatoos, stuffed them into socks, and packed them into suitcases to be smuggled aboard international flights. The birds sold for about $2,500 each on the black market. Caldicott also found out that Australian snakes, other birds, and even **marsupials** were smuggled out of Australia for sale in other countries.

The international trade of smuggled WILDLIFE and wildlife products is a $4 billion- to $5 billion-a-year

◆ Trade in materials made from endangered species is now illegal in many parts of the world.

◆ Poachers will continue to kill endangered animals as long as people continue to offer money for the illegal goods.

the wearing of animal furs and the buying of threatened or endangered species as pets. The United States even has additional laws that allow the president to impose trade sanctions on countries that do not comply with the CITES agreement. Trade sanctions are laws that forbid government officials and citizens of a nation to take part in any business dealings with the nation(s) upon whom the ban is imposed. The United States already imposes such sanctions against countries that violate human rights. Still, the enforcement of CITES requires the cooperation of all involved nations, or the trafficking in endangered animals will not stop until the animals are extinct. [*See also* ANIMAL RIGHTS; ENDANGERED SPECIES ACT; EXOTIC SPECIES; and PET TRADE.]

Convergent Evolution

▶A pattern of EVOLUTION in which distantly related organisms develop similar characteristics over time in response to similar environmental conditions. Convergent evolution can best be explained in terms of the ENVIRONMENT.

Examples of convergent evolution in nature are easy to spot. Think about DOLPHINS and FISH. They are not at all closely related. Dolphins are MAMMALS and are the evolutionary descendants of land animals. Dolphins and fish are separated by hundreds of millions of

business, making it extremely difficult for countries to live up to the CITES agreement. Illegal trade threatens with EXTINCTION large animals like the GIANT PANDA, various REPTILE species, many plants, and many BIRDS. In her book, Caldicott reports on her encounters with professional and nonprofessional smugglers. For example, she tells of a traveler whose luggage was checked in Paris. The luggage contained 50 pythons, 20 tortoises, and

20 lizards. She also describes how a Japanese tourist who landed in Thailand was found to have 11 rare monkeys, 5 of whom had suffocated, jammed into a carry-on bag.

In an effort to reduce the demand for endangered animals and their parts, CONSERVATION groups and the United Nations have pleaded with China and Taiwan to end their centuries-old custom of consuming tiger and rhino parts. Other environmental groups have protested

years of evolution. Nevertheless, these animals have evolved similar shapes because both live in an aquatic HABITAT and face similar conditions in the environment. For example, the streamlined shape and fins and tails of both animals are an adaptive response to the need for moving through water efficiently.

Another example of convergent evolution is seen in marsupial and placental mammals. Marsupials, such as kangaroos and koala bears, are primitive mammals that nourish their young in a marsupium, or external pouch. Most species live in Australia, but some can also be found in South America and North America. Opossums are the only North American marsupial.

Placental mammals, such as dogs, cats, and humans, nourish their young internally through a placenta, a network of blood vessels formed between a developing offspring and its mother. Through the placenta, the growing embryo obtains nutrients, such as food and OXYGEN, and releases wastes. Although both are mammalian groups, marsupials and placentals have evolved independently of one another for at least 100 million years.

What's interesting about placental and marsupial evolution is that, while distantly related, many placental and marsupial species have evolved similar body forms in response to similar environmental factors. For instance, the wolf, a carnivorous placental mammal, has a marsupial counterpart in the Tasmanian wolf. For the placental anteater, there is the marsupial SPECIES, the banded anteater. For the placental field mouse, there is the marsupial mouse.

Marsupial and placental mammals demonstrate that organisms that live in similar environmental conditions can evolve similar ADAPTATIONS. Because convergent evolution occurs between organisms that evolve from entirely different groups of ancestors, it provides strong evidence for NATURAL SELECTION. [*See also* ADAPTIVE RADIATION; BIODIVERSITY; COEVOLUTION; and DARWIN, CHARLES ROBERT.]

◆ Anteater.

◆ Banded anteater.

◆ Mouse.

◆ Marsupial mouse.

◆ Convergent evolution is demonstrated by comparisons between placental and marsupial mammals. Notice the similarities in body form between placentals and their marsupial counterparts.

◆ To operate open-pit copper mines, large areas are cleared, destroying habitats.

◆ Copper mining produces waste materials that can be harmful to the environment.

Copper

▌A brown-red metallic element that is widely used in many metal products. The chemical symbol for copper is Cu.

Copper has five characteristics that make it suitable for many uses. First, it is a good conductor of heat. Second, it is a good conductor of ELECTRICITY. Third, it is resistant to corrosion. Fourth, it can be bent and hammered without breaking. Fifth, it can be drawn into wire.

Copper has been used since prehistoric times to make tools and decorative objects. Today copper is also used to make electrical wires, plumbing pipes, cookware, and many other products. It is also combined with tin to make bronze or with zinc to make brass. In many parts of the world, copper is used in coins.

Copper is removed from Earth's crust through MINING, which can be destructive to the ENVIRONMENT. Many PLANTS are destroyed when bulldozers clear land for mining. The destruction of such plants may disrupt FOOD CHAINS or otherwise disturb the HABITAT of other organisms. In addition, mining can cause POLLUTION. Harmful mine wastes, such as arsenic and sulfur compounds, can be washed into the SOIL and groundwater when it rains. [*See also* HABITAT LOSS and LEACHING.]

Coral Reef

▌A **calcareous** formation, deposited in tropical OCEANS by coral polyps, creating HABITAT for a large and diverse community of marine organisms. Large coral reefs are made by animals that are just fractions of an inch across. These animals are various SPECIES of coral polyps belonging to the phylum Cnidaria. Coral polyps are related to sea anemones and jellyfishes.

Coral polyps have pouch-like bodies, with a "mouth" surrounded by tentacles at the top. The tentacles are used mainly at night for catching PLANKTON. Most polyps are also nourished by single-celled green ALGAE (*zooxanthellae*) that live in their body tissues and manufacture food during the day.

A coral polyp can reproduce in two ways. It can bud a new polyp directly from its own body, or reproduce sexually, so that eggs and sperm unite and develop into larvae. As a polyp grows, specialized cells produce a protective skeleton made of a stonelike substance around it. Over time, this substance can be acted upon by natural processes to form **limestone**. The large amount of limestone deposited by colonies of millions of polyps makes up the foundation of a coral reef.

Most corals grow only where water temperatures do not go below 68° F (20° C). Because algae live in the bodies of the polyps, corals also require light. They do not grow where water is clouded by SEDIMENT or is deeper than about 200 feet (60 meters). Coral reefs are therefore formed in the shallow, warm, and clear waters of the Caribbean, the tropical Indian Ocean, and the tropical Pacific Ocean.

TYPES OF CORAL REEFS

There are several types of coral reefs. *Fringe reefs* form directly off

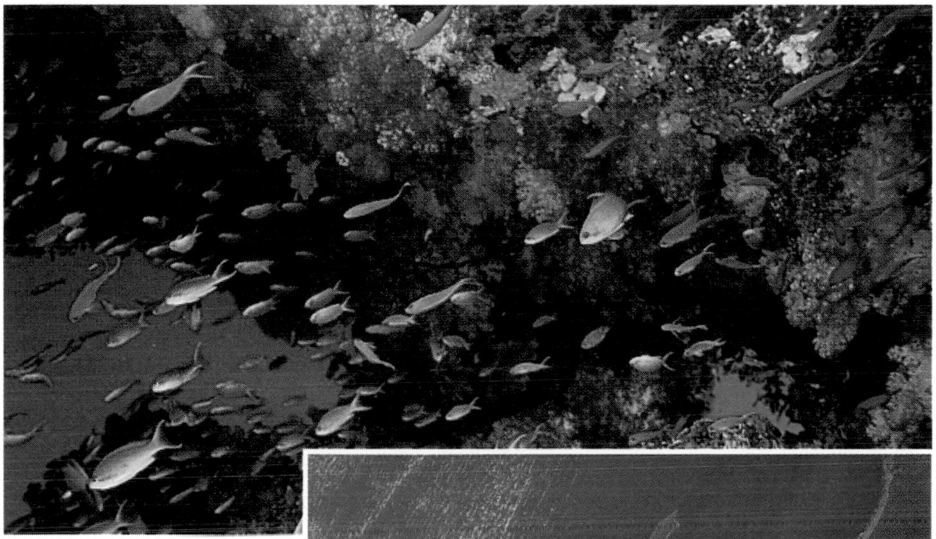

◆ Coral reefs support a diverse community of plants and animals.

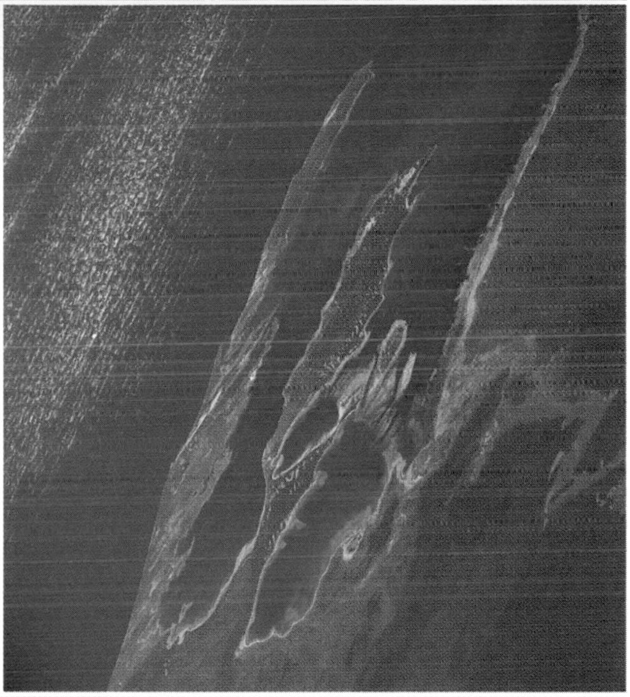

◆ Coral reefs form only in warm and clear waters.

Individual polyps
Tentacles
Mouth
Stomach
Skeleton left
by dead polyp

◆ Tentacles and sticky mucus help coral polyps trap plankton. The soft body of this polyp is usually withdrawn into its hard calcareous skeleton for protection during the day.

THE LANGUAGE OF THE ENVIRONMENT

calcareous containing calcium or compounds of calcium such as calcium carbonate, the main compound in limestone and the shells of corals.

limestone a rock consisting of calcium carbonate, a white powder.

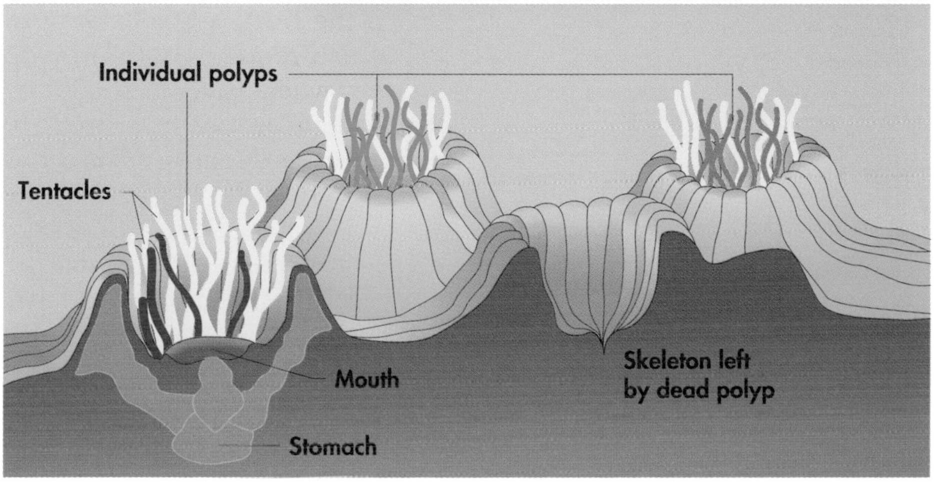

the shores of continents and islands. *Atoll reefs* form at the edges of old submerged volcanoes. They form an irregular ring around a shallow central lagoon, and their outside edges drop steeply to the ocean floor. *Barrier reefs* are platforms of coral that lie just off the shore of an island or continent. Barier reefs form fringe reefs because a barrier reef has a lagoon between land and reef. The largest example of this is the Great Barrier Reef of northeastern Australia, which is 1,240 miles (2,000 kilometers) long and 95 miles (150 kilometers) wide.

As islands and continents subside, or sea levels rise, coral reefs build upward to stay near the

ocean's surface, so that a living reef may sit on top of older layers of dead coral rock. Sometimes this rock is more than 3,300 feet (1,000 meters) thick, showing that these reefs have built up for hundreds of thousands of years.

IMPORTANCE OF CORAL REEFS

Coral reefs are a tropical marine ECOSYSTEM. The open ocean of the tropics is often described as a marine DESERT with few organisms. However, corals and their internal algae trap energy from the sun and nutrients from the water to build complicated structures that provide abundant food and shelter for other organisms. Reef-forming corals thus support many other species, including soft corals; algae; sponges; mollusks (such as snails and giant clams); crustaceans (such as crabs and shrimps); tunicates ("sea squirts"); bryozoans ("moss animals"); many kinds of marine worms; and a great variety of FISH.

Humans also benefit from coral reef ecosystems. The reefs protect tropical coasts from the force of ocean waves, provide food, and are a source of limestone for building or fertilizer. They are also natural laboratories for ecologists who study animal behavior, interactions among species, or the reasons why certain species occur together. Many people also visit coral reefs as underwater tourists.

All these human uses change coral reefs to some extent. In some places, fish communities are greatly depleted by spearfishing, dynamiting, and other forms of overharvesting. MINING and careless use of coral reefs by tourists damage habitat. Silt RUNOFF from human activities on land makes water too cloudy for corals to survive. Similarly, sources of POLLUTION such as OIL SPILLS poison reef communities.

Recently, a phenomenon known as coral reef bleaching has wiped out large areas of the world's coral reefs. Whether this is entirely due to human causes or is one of the natural events that occasionally devastate coral reef is not fully known. However, human-caused damage to these ecosystems is already severe enough to justify concern and protective action. [*See also* BARRIER ISLANDS; BIODIVERSITY; and MARINE PROTECTION, RESEARCH, AND SANCTUARIES ACT.]

Cost-Benefit Analysis

▮A method by which a proposed project is examined to decide if it is worthwhile. A cost-benefit analysis looks at both the financial return on any money invested in a project and any gains or losses the project provides to the people of the community. An example of factors studied in a cost-benefit analysis is weighing the environmental impact of a new industrial plant against the increase in available jobs and added tax revenue for a city. An environmental cost-benefit analysis is similar to a cost-budget analysis used in business.

The use of cost-benefit analysis was first suggested in 1844 by a French engineer. However, the plan was not seriously used until 1936. At that time, the U.S. Flood Control Act required that the advantages of any flood-control proposals be greater than their financial costs. Since the 1960s, cost-benefit analysis has been practiced for most government projects.

COST-BENEFIT RATIO

A project's cost-benefit ratio is decided by dividing the intended benefits of the project by its defined costs. This process is somewhat like trying to divide apples by oranges, because many different variables are involved. These variables are both quantitative and qualitative. For instance, a project's financial gain may not show up for many years. Time is an important factor when estimating costs that frequently change, such as interest rates and wages for employees. When calculating project costs, an organization must consider whether it is wise to tie up available funds

Potential Benefits of Reducing and Preventing Pollution

1. Improved human health and decreased worker stress
2. Increased real estate values
3. Higher profits from improved agricultural and forest production and commercial marine harvests
4. Improved recreational uses, benefiting associated businesses
5. Extended lifetime and reduced maintenance of materials

and disrupt the organization's normal cash flow. Environmental needs change over time, too. For example, if a new industrial plant opens, more people might move to the community to work in the plant. An increase in population creates more tax dollars for the local government, but it also places more stress on NATURAL RESOURCES. In addition, a larger population increases the need for new homes, which creates more construction jobs and increases the amount of tax dollars entering the community. At the same time, the community's need for services such as ELECTRICITY, water, schools, public parks, transportation, and GARBAGE collection also increases. A larger population would probably increase AIR POLLUTION, WATER POLLUTION, and NOISE POLLUTION as well.

OPPONENTS OF COST-BENEFIT ANALYSIS

Critics of cost-benefit analysis insist that it is impossible to determine all advantages in financial terms. They also believe that judging social standards is not the job of those involved in governmental decision-making. These analysts claim that projects designed to help one group may produce unfortunate side effects for other groups. Often, the side effects outweigh the benefits. For example, engineers planning Egypt's Aswan High Dam project in the 1960s concentrated on the need to increase the water supply in the area for IRRIGATION and power. The amount of land to be flooded for the project included an area of 762 miles (1,226 kilometers) south of Cairo, where the Temples of Abu Simbel, commissioned by Pharaoh Ramses II (1304–1237 B.C.), were carved into a sandstone cliff beside the Nile. An international team of engineers and scientists rescued and reconstructed the temples 200 feet (61 meters) above the proposed waterline for the DAM. However, many other **environmental side effects** were not considered. Included in these was the loss of land for the Nile River delta and the spread of a tropical disease called schistosomiasis, which was carried by snails living in the newly provided irrigation ditches.

Some water-development programs supported by international organizations for some semiarid African regions have turned out to be more harmful than helpful. Failure to weigh the ecological and social outcomes of these projects resulted in OVERGRAZING of farmland. The overgrazing, in turn, created DESERTS in areas that were supposed to be improved by money spent in the programs. People involved in the cost-benefit analysis of new projects now recognize the need to request the best environmental advice, but establishing that action as a habit is slow in coming. [*See also* DESERTIFICATION; ENVIRONMENTAL ETHICS; ENVIRONMENTAL IMPACT STATEMENT; LAND USE; NATURAL RESOURCES; and RISK ASSESSMENT.]

THE LANGUAGE OF THE ENVIRONMENT

environmental side effects changes to the environment brought on by human actions to help one segment of the environment. For example, cutting down trees to help a developing nation improve its economy by selling timber to other countries produces side effects such as increased erosion of the stripped timber land, loss of habitat for animals living in the wooded area, and so on.

Council on Environmental Quality (CEQ)

A White House panel that, in the past, advised the president of the United States on environmental issues. The role of the Council on Environmental Quality (CEQ) was greatly diminished during the Reagan and Bush Administrations. President Clinton dismantled the CEQ in 1993 and replaced it with the new White House Office on Environmental Policy. President Clinton said that the new office would "have broader influence and a more effective and focused mandate" than the CEQ.

The CEQ was established in 1969 by the NATIONAL ENVIRONMENTAL POLICY ACT (NEPA) to improve the quality of the ENVIRONMENT. Much of the CEQ's work was making sure that an ENVIRONMENTAL IMPACT STATEMENT was prepared if it was required by law.

Perhaps the CEQ's best-known contribution was the GLOBAL 2000 REPORT. This 1980 report to President Carter was the first to a head of state that made long-term projections about the future of the

environment. "If present trends continue," the report said, "the world in 2000 will be more crowded, more polluted, less stable ecologically and more vulnerable to disruption than the world we live in now." It went on to predict that "the world's people will be poorer in many ways than they are today." The Global 2000 Report had a major impact on U.S. environmental policy. [*See also* COST BENEFIT ANALYSIS; ENVIRONMENTAL AUDITING; and ENVIRONMENTAL PROTECTION AGENCY (EPA).]

Cousteau, Jacques-Yves (1910–)

OCEAN explorer, developer of the Aqualung, pioneer in underwater cinematography, marine biology educator, and advocate for ocean CONSERVATION. Jacques Cousteau was born in Paris, France, in 1910. While he was a boy, the Cousteau family traveled widely and lived in Europe and in New York. Cousteau received most of his education in France—first at the Academy Stanislas and later at the Brest Naval Academy.

Cousteau joined the French navy in 1930 to train as a pilot. However, he was forced out of aviation by injuries received in a car accident. While recovering, he became interested in diving and underwater exploration off the south coast of France. These activities inspired Cousteau and his associates to invent the Aqualung. This device stores compressed air in tanks, carried on a diver's back. It allows the diver to breathe by means of a regulating valve. Today the Aqualung is known by its military name, *scuba,* an acronym for self-contained underwater breathing apparatus.

The Aqualung allowed Cousteau to experiment with another new technology, underwater filming. Cousteau and his film crews were among the first to bring the spectacular sights of the marine world to a wide audience. His first short film, *Par dix-huit mètres de fond (At a Depth of Eighteen Meters),* was produced in 1942. In

1956, his first full-length color film, *Le monde du silence (The World of Silence),* won international acclaim. Cousteau created several other films and television programs, from the 1950s through the 1980s. All of these presented information about marine exploration and ecology to the general public, while enhancing the popularity of research in marine biology. During the same period, Cousteau authored or coauthored dozens of popular books and magazine articles on marine life.

In the 1960s and 1970s, Cousteau crusaded to warn people about the effects of ocean POLLUTION and the overharvesting of marine organisms. He urged that restrictions be placed on the dumping of high-level waste and other ocean pollutants. Cousteau also recommended less exploitive approaches to fishing. Around this time, Cousteau experimented with housing humans for extended periods in undersea work stations and promoted high-technology approaches to using ocean resources more efficiently.

The Cousteau Society, a nonprofit organization that supports Cousteau's work, was founded in 1974. The work of the Cousteau Society has grown over time. At its founding, the main goals of the society were to observe marine life and popularize marine research. Today it actively participates in solving social and political problems that threaten the oceans and other ECOSYSTEMS. [*See also* FISHING, COMMERCIAL; MARINE POLLUTION; MEAD, SYLVIA EARLE; and OCEAN DUMPING.]

Crop Rotation

▶The practice of alternating different farm plants on a plot of land. Crop rotation is a traditional farming practice that helps prevent nutrients in the SOIL from being depleted. It relies on the fact that some crop PLANTS rapidly use up

◆ Planting crops side by side is one way of naturally fertilizing the soil.

important nutrients from the soil while other plants help add nutrients. For instance, cotton, corn, and wheat quickly use up available nutrients in the soil, especially nitrogen. On the other hand, LEGUMES, such as soybeans and alfalfa, add nitrogen to the soil. Alternating, or rotating, crops in a field helps assure that the soil will always stay fertile.

HOW CROP ROTATION WORKS

Farmers who use crop rotation plant a series of different crops over the course of several growing seasons. For example, a farmer might begin with a nutrient-adding plant, such as alfalfa. Alfalfa would be grown for three seasons. The plants

◆ Soybean is a legume that provides the soil with nutrients needed by the corn planted beside it.

would be plowed back into the soil after each season to enrich it with nutrients. Next, over the course of four growing seasons, a farmer might plant wheat, then soybeans, then wheat again, and finally oats. After this, the rotation would be started again. In this sequence, the nutrient adding crops (alfalfa and soybeans) fertilize the soil so wheat can be grown.

ENVIRONMENTAL ISSUES

Crop rotation is an important part of ORGANIC FARMING and SUSTAINABLE AGRICULTURE practices. In addition to keeping soils fertile, crop rotation helps reduce pest problems. Since crops are rotated every season, pest populations that infest certain plants are not allowed to build up over many years. Crop rotation thus reduces the need for synthetic PESTICIDES and fertilizers that can harm the ENVIRONMENT. [*See also* AGRO-ECOLOGY; INSECTICIDES; NITROGEN CYCLE; NITROGEN FIXING; and SOIL CONSERVATION.]

Curbside Recycling

See RECYCLING, REDUCING, REUSING